Life in a Japanese American Internment Camp

Titles in The Way People Live series include:

Cowboys in the Old West
Life Among the Great Plains Indians
Life Among the Indian Fighters
Life During the Crusades
Life During the French Revolution
Life During the Great Depression
Life During the Renaissance
Life During the Russian Revolution
Life During the Spanish Inquisition
Life in a Japanese American Internment Camp
Life in Ancient Greece
Life in Ancient Rome
Life in an Eskimo Village
Life in the Elizabethan Theater
Life in the North During the Civil War
Life in the South During the Civil War
Life in the Warsaw Ghetto
Life in War-Torn Bosnia
Life on a Medieval Pilgrimage
Life on an Israeli Kibbutz

THE WAY
PEOPLE
LIVE

Life in a Japanese American Internment Camp

by Diane Yancey

Lucent Books, P.O. Box 289011, San Diego, CA 92198-9011

9341090

Library of Congress Cataloging-in-Publication Data

Yancey, Diane.
    Life in a Japanese American internment camp / by Diane Yancey.
      p.   cm. — (The Way people live)
    Includes bibliographical references and index.
    Summary: Discusses the course of Japanese immigration into the United
States, events leading to the relocation of Japanese Americans during World
War II, and the conditions they faced in the internment camps.
    ISBN 1-56006-345-9 (alk. paper)
    1. Japanese Americans—Evacuation and relocation, 1942–1945.
2. World War, 1939–1945—Concentration camps—United States.
3. World War, 1939–1945—Personal narratives, American.
[1. Japanese Americans—Evacuation and relocation, 1942–1945.]
I. Title.   II. Series.
D769.8.A6Y36   1998
940.53'1773—dc21

                                           97-21422
                                               CIP
                                               AC

Printed in the U.S.A.

Contents

Discovering the Humanity in Us All

The Way People Live series focuses on pockets of human culture. Some of these are current cultures, like the Eskimos of the Arctic; others no longer exist, such as the Jewish ghetto in Warsaw during World War II. What many of these cultural pockets share, however, is the fact that they have been viewed before, but not completely understood.

To really understand any culture, it is necessary to strip the mind of the common notions we hold about groups of people. These stereotypes are the archenemies of learning. It does not even matter whether the stereotypes are positive or negative; they are confining and tight. Removing them is a challenge that's not easily met, as anyone who has ever tried it will admit. Ideas that do not fit into the templates we create are unwelcome visitors—ones we would prefer remain quietly in a corner or forgotten room.

The cowboy of the Old West is a good example of such confining roles. The cowboy was courageous, yet soft-spoken. His time (it is always a he, in our template) was spent alternatively saving a rancher's daughter from certain death on a runaway stagecoach, or shooting it out with rustlers. At times, of course, he was likely to get a little crazy in town after a trail drive, but for the most part, he was the epitome of inner strength. It is disconcerting to find out that the cowboy is human, even a bit childish. Can it really be true that cowboys would line up to help the cook on the trail drive grind coffee, just hoping he would give them a little stick of pep-

permint candy that came with the coffee shipment? The idea of tough cowboys vying with one another to help "Coosie" (as they called their cooks) for a bit of candy seems silly and out of place.

So is the vision of Eskimos playing video games and watching MTV, living in prefab housing in the Arctic. It just does not fit with what "Eskimo" means. We are far more comfortable with snow igloos and whale blubber, harpoons and kayaks.

Although the cultures dealt with in Lucent's The Way People Live series are often historically and socially well known, the emphasis is on the personal aspects of life. Groups of people, while unquestionably affected by their politics and their governmental structures, are more than those institutions. How do people in a particular time and place educate their children? What do they eat? And how do they build their houses? What kinds of work do they do? What kinds of games do they enjoy? The answers to these questions bring these cultures to life. People's lives are revealed in the particulars and only by knowing the particulars can we understand these cultures' will to survive and their moments of weakness and greatness.

This is not to say that understanding politics does not help to understand a culture. There is no question that the Warsaw ghetto, for example, was a culture that was brought about by the politics and social ideas of Adolf Hitler and the Third Reich. But the Jews who were crowded together in the ghetto cannot be understood by the Reich's politics. Their life was a day-to-day battle for existence, and the creativity and methods they used to prolong their lives is a vital story of human perseverance that would be denied by focusing only on the institutions of Hitler's Germany. Knowing that children as young as five or six outwitted Nazi guards on a daily basis, that Jewish policemen helped the Germans control the ghetto, that children attended secret schools in the ghetto and even earned diplomas—these are the things that reveal the fabric of life, that can inspire, intrigue, and amaze.

Books in the The Way People Live series allow both the casual reader and the student to see humans as victims, heroes, and onlookers. And although humans act in ways that can fill us with feelings of sorrow and revulsion, it is important to remember that "hero," "predator," and "victim" are dangerous terms. Heaping undue pity or praise on people reduces them to objects, and strips them of their humanity.

Seeing the Jews of Warsaw only as victims is to deny their humanity. Seeing them only as they appear in surviving photos, staring at the camera with infinite sadness, is limiting, both to them and to those who want to understand them. To an object of pity, the only appropriate response becomes "Those poor creatures!" and that reduces both the quality of their struggle and the depth of their despair. No one is served by such two-dimensional views of people and their cultures.

With this in mind, the The Way People Live series strives to flesh out the traditional, two-dimensional views of people in various cultures and historical circumstances. Using a wide variety of primary quotations—the words not only of the politicians and government leaders, but of the real people whose lives are being examined—each book in the series attempts to show an honest and complete picture of a culture removed from our own by time or space.

By examining cultures in this way, the reader will notice not only the glaring differences from his or her own culture, but also will be struck by the similarities. For indeed, people share common needs—warmth, good company, stability, and affirmation from others. Ultimately, seeing how people really live, or have lived can only enrich our understanding of ourselves.

The "Quiet Americans"

They thought of themselves as Americans, despite their Asian faces, their foreign-sounding names, and their Japanese ancestry. Like most Americans, they worked hard all week and went to church on Sunday. Their children rode bicycles, chewed bubble gum, and solemnly pledged allegiance to the flag at school every morning.

With the rest of America, they listened to their radios on December 7, 1941, when the announcement was made that Japanese planes had attacked the U.S. fleet anchored at Pearl Harbor, Hawaii. To their horror, they learned that American battleships and planes had been destroyed and thousands of American lives had been lost. When President Franklin Delano Roosevelt declared war against Japan a day later, most loyally supported the decision.

A Fact of Life

But Japanese Americans (a term used for all Japanese living in America) knew that they were not seen as true Americans by their white neighbors, despite the many similarities in lifestyle and outlook. Racial discrimination against Asians was a fact of life on the West Coast (where most Japanese lived), particularly since Japanese laborers and farmers were ambitious and hardworking, and many Caucasian businessmen and landowners feared that they would take white jobs and put white Americans out of work. Before Pearl Harbor, federal law already limited Japanese immigration into the United States

A paperboy hawks newspapers in the wake of the December 7, 1941, attack on Pearl Harbor.

and prohibited Japanese nationals from becoming U.S. citizens, from owning land, and from voting.

The outbreak of war brought a noticeable intensification of public feeling against Japanese Americans. Whites on the West Coast who lived in fear of a Japanese attack now viewed their Japanese neighbors with increased hatred and fear, suspecting that, as a group, all were loyal to Japan. Japanese Americans were regularly accused of being spies, of planning to sabotage military bases, and of sending military secrets to Japan. As one columnist wrote on January 4, 1942:

It would be extremely foolish to doubt the continued existence of enemy agents among the large alien Japanese population [in California]. Only recently city health inspectors looking over a Japanese rooming house came upon a powerful [radio] transmitter, and it is reasonable to assume that menace of a similar character must be constantly guarded against throughout the war.[1]

Such reports were usually groundless, but they caused widespread fear. "We recommend the immediate evacuation of all persons of Japanese lineage," urged Representative Clarence Lea, speaking on behalf of congressmen in California, Oregon, and Washington in early 1942. "We make these recommendations in order that no citizen, located in a strategic area, may cloak his disloyalty or subversive activity under the mantle of his citizenship."[2]

A Devastating Blow

Official reaction against Japanese Americans peaked in February 1942 with President Roosevelt's signing of Executive Order 9066, a directive authorizing the removal of all people of Japanese ancestry from the western United States. By the end of 1942, virtually the entire Japanese American population on the West Coast—more than 110,000 men, women, and children—had been relocated to internment camps throughout the country.

Seventy percent were American citizens, born in the United States and supposedly protected by law from unjust imprisonment.

Employees and patrons of the Liberty Cafe in Boston, Massachusetts, point to a sign in the window proclaiming, "No Japs served here." Following the Pearl Harbor attack, many Americans began discriminating against Japanese Americans.

They and their families lost jobs, property, and possessions as a result of the relocation. The most devastating blow, however, was the humiliation all experienced as they were wrenched out of society and locked like criminals in bleak, overcrowded prison camps. "Since yesterday we Japanese have ceased to be human beings," Hatsuye Egami wrote in his diary. "We are numbers. We are no longer Egamis, but the number 23324. A tag with that number is on every trunk, suitcase and bag. Tags, also, on our breasts."[3]

Despite such dehumanizing treatment, most internees worked hard to control their bitterness, to create workable communities inside the camps, and to continue to be the good citizens they had always been. They were so successful that, after release came in 1945, they became known as the "model minority," admired both for their skill in reintegrating into mainstream society and for their continued determination to be loyal Americans.

A Terrible Mistake

The internment of Japanese American citizens has come to be described by one army official as a "mistake of terrifically horrible proportions."[4] Yet even after the mistake was acknowledged by government officials, formal apologies and compensation for personal losses were slow in coming. Ironically, the delay was in part due to the fact that the internees themselves did not demand justice. "We have

The Mochida family somberly poses for a photograph while waiting to board evacuation buses. Tags identifying their family by a designated number hang from the lapels of the children's coats.

Life in America

The internees did what they could to bring order and purpose to their days, often by introducing typical American activities, as one young internee explains in Personal Justice Denied, *a report compiled by the Commission on Wartime Relocation and Internment of Civilians.*

"In some ways, I suppose, my life was not too different from a lot of kids in America between the years 1942 and 1945. I spent a good part of my time playing with my brothers and friends, learned to shoot marbles, watched sandlot baseball and envied the older kids who wore Boy Scout uniforms. We shared with the rest of America the same movies, screen heroes and listened to the same heartrending songs of the forties. We imported much of America into the camps because, after all, we were Americans. Through imitation of my brothers, who attended grade school within the camp, I learned the salute to the flag by the time I was five years old. I was learning, as best one could learn in Manzanar, what it meant to live in America. But, I was also learning the sometimes bitter price one has to pay for it."

always been told that we are the 'Quiet Americans,'" says Martha Yoshioka, a former internee. "We think a lot in our own mind, but we don't say it with our words, because we don't like to make too many waves."[5]

Yet the internees could not forget their war experience. As time passed, many felt compelled to speak of this dark period of U.S. history—of government betrayal, of life in the camps, and of their reaction to an unjust imprisonment. They wanted to share their painful experiences and their insights with others. They wanted to guard against such an injustice ever happening again. As former internee Mary Tsukamoto says:

I know many . . . who say, That was all so long ago. Let's forget it and leave well enough alone. But I just say, we were the ones that went through it—the tears and the shame and the shock. We need to leave our legacy to our children. And also our legacy to America, from our tears, what we learned.[6]

Latecomers to America

Despite the welcoming words on the Statue of Liberty—"Give me your tired, your poor, your huddled masses yearning to breathe free"—almost all immigrants face some form of discrimination when they arrive in the United States. Americans not only distrust outsiders who look and act different, many Caucasian Americans are convinced that "white brains and power" are always superior to those of other races. African Americans, Hispanics, Native Americans, Jews, even southern Europeans were considered inferior and therefore less welcome in business, in neighborhoods, and at social functions. The Japanese were no exception, as the Commission on Wartime Relocation and Internment of Civilians, formed in 1980 to investigate Japanese American internment, reported. "Whatever the reasons or motives, much of the country believed in fundamental racial differences and practiced those beliefs through some form of discrimination or segregation."[7]

The Yellow Flood: Asians Come to America

Anti-Asian feeling in the United States was first directed against the Chinese, who arrived in America before the Japanese. Along with thousands of other hopeful prospectors, the Chinese came to California in the 1850s looking for gold, although hundreds also came to work on the railroads. Many eventually settled on the West Coast and established small businesses such as laundries and restaurants. By 1870 Chinese numbered over sixty thousand in the United States and made up approximately 10 percent of California's population.

Not surprisingly, white Americans felt threatened by this influx of Oriental immigrants, although their numbers were small compared with the millions of Europeans arriving on the East Coast during this period. Not only did Chinese look different with their pigtails, pajama-like clothing, and Oriental faces, they worked longer hours for lower wages than whites. Soon Western politicians, worried about white unemployment, were calling for a ban on Chinese immigration, which they called the "yellow flood." An agreement that halted the inflow of Chinese for ten years became law in 1882, during Chester Arthur's presidency. The ban became permanent in 1902 and was only fully repealed in 1952.

Supported by legislation, discrimination against Chinese was open and acceptable. Chinese were barred from jobs and forbidden to testify in courts. They were robbed, assaulted on the street, and, at times, murdered by white mobs. As historian Roger Daniels writes in his book *Concentration Camps U.S.A.*, "the whole anti-Chinese episode in our history served as a kind of prophetic prologue for what would befall immigrants from Japan."[8]

New Opportunities

Around 1890 Japanese immigrants began arriving in America for the same reasons other immigrants had come in the past—freedom, economic opportunity, and the promise of a better life. During a peak period between 1901 and 1908, 125,000 Japanese immigrants arrived and settled on the West Coast. Most were young men from the Japanese countryside, intent on working hard and making their fortunes. Times were hard in Japan, as one newcomer explained:

> I grew up in a farm in Japan. My father owned a fairly large piece of land, but it was heavily mortgaged. I remember how hard we all had to work, and I also remember the hard times. I saw little future in farm work . . . so at my first good chance I went to work in Osaka. Later I came to California and worked as a laborer in all kinds of jobs.[9]

Many of these immigrants had every intention of returning to Japan, but since most deeply admired America and saw great benefits in living here, they soon changed their minds about leaving. One immigrant, Raymond Katagi, explained: "As they lived long in this country, they found out it is a good place to live, and their descendants

Chinese laborers help construct the transcontinental railroad. During the 1850s, hundreds of Chinese immigrants came to America in search of work; by 1870 over sixty thousand Chinese lived in the United States.

This illustration captures some of the brutalities committed against the Chinese during the 1880s. In addition to their property being destroyed, many Chinese were beaten, robbed, and had their pigtails cut off by rowdy mobs.

have so much more opportunity in this country so they want their descendants . . . to stay in this country, and they have the same ideas as those pilgrim fathers." [10]

Issei

Beginning near the bottom rung of the economic scale, the new immigrants (known as Issei, first-generation Japanese in America) concentrated on learning English and adapting to life in the United States as quickly as possible. Laws barred them from working in manufacturing, construction, and other similar jobs, so they turned to those occupations that were open to them. Remaining in the West, particularly in California, many Issei set up small businesses similar to those of the Chinese: laundries, restaurants, curio shops. Some purchased their own boats and became commercial fishermen. A great many leased land and became truck farmers, growing vegetables, fruits, and flowers that they marketed in nearby cities.

Practicing what were popularly thought of as "Puritan traits"—honesty, hard work, dependability, and thrift—the Issei gradually improved their lot in their adopted country. One of the most successful rags-to-riches stories was that of George Shima, an immigrant who came to the United States in 1889. Shima first worked as a laborer, then a labor contractor. He then invested his profits in land, and went on to build an agricultural empire in California. Known as "the Potato King," he eventually controlled 85 percent of California's potato crop, and employed more than five hundred persons, many of them white laborers. At his death in 1926, his estate was estimated at $15 million. The pallbearers at his funeral included the mayor of San Francisco and the chancellor of Stanford University.

"They Worked Wonders"

No doubt George Shima's success was extraordinary, but thousands of other Japanese achieved a measure of economic well-being through hard work and perseverance, as well. Using the farming skills they had learned in Japan, many reclaimed swampland, wasteland, and small strips along railroads and power lines that had been scorned by white farmers. Drawing on their knowledge of irrigation, fertilizers, and crop rotation, these farmers were able to produce an abundance of crops that few Caucasian farmers grew—strawberries, lettuce, celery, and melons, to name a few. Author John Hersey writes, "They . . . worked wonders with the soil. They owned about one-fiftieth of the arable land in the three coast states, and what they had made of their farms is suggested by the fact that the average value per acre of all

Emigrants from Japan arrive in San Francisco harbor on July 25, 1920. Like the Chinese immigrants before them, the Japanese hoped to find a more prosperous life in America.

farms in the three states in 1940 was $37.94, while an acre on a [Japanese American] farm was worth . . . $279.96."[11]

Anti-Japanese Fears

Many whites in the West watched in amazement and chagrin as Japanese immigrants moved up the economic scale from poverty to middle-class status. Reaction was predictably negative. Unions barred them from membership and from work in some trades. School boards discussed segregation, and a few implemented it. Newspapers wrote about the Japanese "problem," arguing that the new immigrants were threatening the prosperity of the country and endangering the safety of American citizens. Headlines read: "Japanese a Menace to American Women," and "The Yellow Peril—How Japanese Crowd Out the White Race." Mayor James Duval Phelan of San Francisco expressed the mood of the times. "The Japanese are starting the same tide of immigration which we thought we had checked twenty years ago. . . . The Chinese and Japanese are not bona fide citizens. They are not the stuff of which American citizens

During the early 1900s, anti-Japanese sentiment coursed through the nation. Particularly in the West, whites feared that Japanese immigrants would take jobs from American citizens.

are made. . . . [L]et them keep at a respectful distance."[12]

In 1905, as an outgrowth of such attitudes, the Japanese Exclusion League (also known as the Asiatic Exclusion League) was founded in San Francisco, made up of dozens of business interests whose goal it was to exclude the Japanese. The league was joined by other anti-Japanese organizations such as the Native Sons (and Daughters) of the Golden West, the American Legion, and the California State Grange, all of which believed that Japanese laborers were putting Caucasians out of work. In fact, few Japanese businesses competed directly with white businesses; many catered exclusively to the Japanese.

The Gentlemen's Agreement

By 1905 the West's anti-Japanese movement was making itself heard in Washington, D.C., as well. Earlier legislation already prohibited Japanese (and other Asian immigrants) from becoming citizens and from voting. Now, however, the three major political parties—Republicans, Democrats, and Populists—began calling for an end to all Asian immigration into the United States.

At the time, however, Japan was a relatively strong military power, and President Theodore Roosevelt hesitated to offend its leaders by closing his country to Japanese immigrants. Such a move might even precipitate war. Thus, in 1907 Roosevelt took a more subtle approach to settling the problem, negotiating with Japan what became known as the Gentlemen's Agreement of 1907–1908. Under its terms, the Japanese government agreed to stop issuing passports to laborers and to restrict immigration to "laborers who have already been in America and to the parents, wives, and children of

Three young Japanese immigrants pose for a photograph upon their arrival at Angel Island, California, in 1920. Although the Gentlemen's Agreement restricted immigration, it was not a total ban; families of Japanese laborers already in the United States were allowed to immigrate.

laborers already resident there."[13] In return the United States would stop passing anti-Japanese legislation and would allow limited immigration to continue.

Picture Brides

Ironically, the Gentlemen's Agreement increased rather than decreased the number of Japanese coming to the West Coast. Many Japanese immigrants had left wives and families behind when they came to America. Now, those women and children had a legal right to enter the country, and tens of thousands of them did so.

Picture brides are photographed as they arrive in San Francisco in 1912. These young women made the long journey to the United States to join their Japanese husbands who were already in the country.

So did the so-called picture brides, young Japanese women who agreed to enter into arranged marriages with Japanese immigrants already living in the United States. Although many unmarried Japanese returned to Japan to marry and escort their new wives back to America, some men who had immigrated to the United States could not afford the trip. Instead, parents in Japan would carefully pick out a girl who they felt would be suitable for their son. The prospective bride and groom would exchange pictures, and if both liked what they saw, the young couple would then marry, usually by proxy (someone would stand in for the groom during the ceremony). Shortly thereafter, the new bride set sail for America to join her new husband.

Author Yoshiko Uchida, whose mother had taken part in a similarly arranged mar-

riage, describes the bravery of these young women who came alone to a new life and a new land:

> I believe those early Issei women must have had tremendous reserves of strength and courage to do what they did, often masked by their quiet and unassertive demeanor. They came to an alien land, created homes for their men, worked beside them in fields, small shops, and businesses, and at the same time bore most of the responsibility for raising their children. Theirs was a determination and endurance born, I would say, of an uncommon spirit.[14]

White Americans were predictably dismayed by the arrival of the picture brides.

First, arranged marriages, although relatively common in Japan, seemed outlandish to Americans, who believed it was proper to first meet and fall in love. Next, many Westerners suddenly realized that the Gentlemen's Agreement was not a total ban on Japanese immigration as they had assumed. (Not until Congress passed the National Origins Act in 1924 was such a ban in place.) Finally, the arrival of the brides marked the beginning of Japanese American families. Over one hundred thousand Japanese already lived in California, Washington, and Oregon, and that number was rapidly increasing as more and more Japanese American children were born.

Nisei

The fact that the picture brides promptly began having children infuriated many Americans. These children, known as Nisei—the first generation to be born in America—were automatically U.S. citizens according to law. (Before 1924, Nisei were also automatically Japanese citizens because of their ancestry, but after that date, Issei parents had to register their children in Japan if they desired such dual citizenship. Most parents did not make the effort.)

Through their children, the Issei now could take advantage of some of the rights and privileges they had been so long denied. One of the most important was the right to own land. The Alien Land Law of 1913 barred purchases of land by immigrants who could not become citizens (i.e., Issei), so only a small number had managed to buy land, using the name of a cooperative Caucasian friend or an older Nisei to get around the law. "After I was 21," Ichiro Yamaguchi remembered, "being one of the older nisei, I had to buy land for other people. . . . When people asked me to help them this way, I never refused. I would sign all the papers and they made all the payments."[15] Once the Issei had their own children, however, the process became simpler and less expensive. More and more Issei were able to buy land in the name of a "citizen child," and appoint themselves guardians if that child was a minor.

Americanized!

Growing up in America, the Nisei were a blend of Japanese and American cultures. They were raised by Issei parents who identified with and retained strong ties to Japan, and exposed their children to its traditions. The Issei spoke Japanese, lived in Japanese communities, and kept their Japanese manners and customs. Like all traditional Japanese, they demanded strict obedience from their children and expected them to conform to authority and to community standards.

Most young Nisei understood and tolerated these Japanese customs and traditions but did not follow them closely. The Nisei were native to America and as comfortable with its ways as other American children. Schools fostered this Western outlook. In school, Nisei teens spoke American slang just as millions of other American teens did. Like their Caucasian friends, they dressed in jeans and bobby socks, danced the jitterbug, and enjoyed hamburgers and soft drinks. Yoshiko Uchida, a Nisei herself, explains:

In spite of the complete blending of Japanese qualities and values into our lives, neither my sister nor I, as children, ever considered ourselves anything other than Americans. At school we saluted the American flag and learned to become good citizens. All our teachers were white, as were many of our friends. Everything we read was in English, which was, of course, our native tongue.[16]

The exception among young Japanese Americans were the Kibei, so called because, although born in America, they had been sent by their parents to Japan for a portion of their education. Many Kibei thought more like the Issei; they were more loyal to Japan and less comfortable in white society than the Nisei.

A Serious Obstacle

A Japanese child could not go to American schools and mix in American society without encountering prejudice and discrimination. Despite the fact that the Nisei worked hard and stayed out of trouble, they were regular-ly excluded from contests, ignored by waiters and store clerks, and turned away from public swimming pools and dances because of their race. Taught by their parents to be polite and to cause no trouble, many coped with such unfair treatment by developing a cautious approach to everyday experiences, as Yoshiko Uchida describes:

When I had outgrown my father's home haircuts and wanted to go to a beauty parlor, I telephoned first to ask if they would take me.

"Do you cut Japanese hair?"

"Can we come swim in the pool? We're Japanese."

"Will you rent us a house? Will the neighbors object?"

Unwarranted Shame

Instead of rebelling against the prejudice they faced at school and work every day, many young Japanese Americans internalized that prejudice and came to see themselves as an inferior race. Yoshiko Uchida, who lived with her parents in San Francisco prior to internment, describes this unwarranted shame in her book Desert Exile.

"Society caused us to feel ashamed of something that should have made us feel proud. Instead of directing anger at the society that excluded and diminished us, such was the climate of the times and so low our self-esteem that many of us Nisei tried to reject our own Japaneseness and the Japanese ways of our parents. We were sometimes ashamed of the Issei in their shabby clothes, their run down trucks and cars, their skin darkened from years of laboring in sun-parched fields, their inability to speak English, their habits, and the food they ate.

I would be embarrassed when my mother behaved in what seemed to me a non-American way. I would cringe when I was with her as she met a Japanese friend on the street and began a series of bows, speaking all the while in Japanese.

'Come on, Mama,' I would interrupt, tugging at her sleeve. 'Let's go,' I would urge, trying to terminate the long exchange of amenities. I felt disgraced in public."

Schoolchildren in San Francisco recite the "Pledge of Allegiance" while a Japanese American student proudly holds the American flag. Although born in the United States, Nisei children faced discrimination and prejudice in both American schools and society.

These were the kinds of questions we asked in order to avoid embarrassment and humiliation.[17]

Many Nisei became model citizens and high achievers, not only to satisfy themselves but to prove to white Americans that they were worthy of acceptance. Still, prejudice kept them from achieving the success they had earned. Nisei who graduated with high honors from colleges and universities could not find work as teachers. Premed students were refused places in medical schools. Fully-trained design engineers had to settle for jobs as grocery boys or clerks in gift shops. As one young Nisei wrote in 1937: "I am a fruitstand worker. It is not a very attractive nor distinguished occupation. . . . I would much rather it were doctor or lawyer . . . but my aspiration of developing into such (was) frustrated long ago. . . . I am only what I am, a professional carrot washer."[18]

"Real Americans"

Discrimination wounded many young Nisei deeply, but rather than protest and grow bitter, they worked harder to prove their loyalty to and support for all things American. Some joined the military. Some formed all-Japanese Young Republican and Young Democrat political parties. Others founded all-Japanese American Legion posts. In 1930 leaders of a number of local and regional groups came together and founded the

Anti-Japanese Sentiment

Japan's aggressiveness, including its invasion of China and the bombing of the American gunboat Panay, *was widely known throughout the world by the 1930s. The flames of anti-Japanese sentiment had been fanned by patriotic organizations and elements of the American press even earlier than that, however, as the authors of* Personal Justice Denied *explain.*

"Popular writing, the movies, and the Hearst newspapers in particular, promoted the fear. 'Patria,' produced by Hearst's International Film Service Corp. in 1917, and 'Shadows of the West,' circulated by the American Legion, both portrayed Japanese immigrants as sneaky, treacherous agents of a militaristic Japan seeking to control the West Coast. Two novels written by the respected Peter B. Kyne and Wallace Irwin about dangers of Japanese land ownership were serialized in the *Saturday Evening Post* and Hearst's *Cosmopolitan*. Pseudoscientific literature began to discuss the inferiority of Eastern and Southern European stock as well as the 'yellow people.' Madison Grant's 1917 work *The Passing of the Great Race* argued that immigration was 'mongrelizing' America. . . .

Purported [alleged] espionage by those of Japanese ancestry in the United States was advanced as one threat from the yellow peril. Allegations that persons of Japanese descent were a 'secret army' for Japan and the Emperor were constantly repeated by anti-Japanese agitators."

Japanese American Citizens League (JACL), which limited its membership to citizens, stressed Americanization, and minimized ties with Japan. As tension between the United States and Japan grew in the 1930s, members of the JACL went out of their way to prove that they were "real Americans" by cooperating with the Federal Bureau of Investigation (FBI) and military intelligence. The JACL's creed, written by Nisei Mike Masaoka sometime in 1940, expressed the almost super-Americanism felt by many of its members:

> I am proud that I am an American citizen of Japanese ancestry, for my very background makes me appreciate more fully the wonderful advantages of this nation. I believe in her institutions, ideals and traditions; I glory in her heritage; I boast of her history; I trust in her future.[19]

The JACL's creed reflected the optimism and high expectations many young Nisei felt for themselves and the United States. The chilling events of December 1941, however, dampened even the most optimistic spirits and proved to the Nisei that they had misjudged their country. Too many white Americans did not listen to or believe any Japanese American's proclamation of loyalty. As historian Roger Daniels points out, "When the chips were down their countrymen saw only the color of their skin and remembered only that their parents had come from the land of the rising sun."[20]

"What Is Going to Happen to Us?"

The bombing of Pearl Harbor on December 7, 1941, stunned Japanese Americans just as it stunned millions of others across the United States. Many had scoffed at the idea that a tiny nation like Japan would dare attack a world power. Others had believed that the United States would be able to foresee any Japanese strike and would therefore take steps to prevent or defeat it.

With the surprise attack and the president's declaration of war, however, Japanese Americans could not help but worry. All knew that many white Americans believed them to be loyal to their homeland and its emperor. Now that Japan and America were at war, they were unsure what the future would hold.

Reaction to Suspicion

The Issei, who were Japanese citizens and could possibly be suspect, reacted with fear. Many hastily destroyed anything they owned that might be judged suspicious or disloyal—Japanese flags, samurai swords, and books in Japanese—even if those possessions were cherished family mementos. After that, they stayed off the street, listened to their radios, and waited.

The Nisei were cautious but more confident. They were U.S. citizens. America was their country; nothing bad could happen to them there. To prove their loyalty, many went out and purchased war bonds. Some joined the Red Cross; others volunteered for civilian defense patrols. A number of young men decided to join the military even before they were drafted. Jack Tono, a Nisei born in San Jose, remembers, "All being citizens, a bunch of us were talking that we eventually would have to go. Go to the Army and defend the country, that was about the main thing." [21] And Charles Kikuchi, a Nisei college student living in San Francisco, wrote in his diary:

> Pearl Harbor. We are at war! . . . The Japs bombed Hawaii and the entire fleet has been sunk. I just can't believe it. I don't know what . . . is going to happen to us, but we will all be called into the Army right away. . . . I will go and fight even if I think I am a coward and I don't believe in wars. . . . If we are ever going to prove our Americanism, this is the time. [22]

Pro-Japanese?

Many Americans, especially those on the West Coast, believed that there was good reason to question the loyalty of Japanese Americans. For instance, a great number of Issei belonged to *kenjinkai*, traditional Japanese associations made up of people from the same *ken,* or clan. Other Issei were involved in patriotic organizations, known as *kai*, that professed loyalty to Japan. Members of the Heimisha Kai in San Francisco regularly collected funds to be sent to Japan to help the

Men of all ages and races registered for the draft after the United States entered the war in 1941. Many Nisei supported the war effort by joining the military or volunteering for the Red Cross or civilian defense patrol.

War Ministry. The Togo Kai was named after a hero of the Russo-Japanese War; its purpose was to collect funds for the Japanese navy.

In addition to membership in Japanese organizations, many Issei subscribed to newspapers printed in Japanese containing news of the homeland. They sent their children to Japanese language schools to ensure they could speak Japanese. Some Japanese Americans even celebrated holidays that involved worship of the Japanese emperor, who was traditionally considered a god in Japan.

In the eyes of white Americans, such pro-Japanese associations indicated loyalty to Japan. It seemed logical that those who were loyal to Japan would be anti-American, willing to express their animosity through sabotage and espionage.

Loyal to America

Americans need not have worried so much about the Japanese in their midst. Only a few

months before Pearl Harbor, a State Department official, Curtis B. Munson, had filed a report that included information on possible danger from West Coast Japanese. Munson found that, although the Pacific states were poorly protected against enemy attack, the great majority of Japanese Americans were wholeheartedly loyal to America and posed no threat in time of war. Munson pointed out that the physical characteristics of Japanese would make them easily identifiable if they attempted undercover work, and noted that few had the opportunity to spy or commit sabotage. "The Japanese here is almost exclusively a farmer, a fisherman or a small business man. He has no entree to plants or intricate machinery,"[23] he wrote.

Munson's report was the result of interviews with army and naval intelligence officers, businessmen, university professors, farmers, and religious groups on the West Coast. Had it been widely published, fears about Japanese Americans might have been dispelled. "As interview after interview piled up," Munson wrote, "those bringing in results began to call it the same old tune. . . . There is no Japanese 'problem' on the Coast. There will be no armed uprising of Japanese."[24]

Unfortunately, Munson's report remained almost secret, as were similar reports filed by Kenneth D. Ringle, one of several naval officers stationed in southern California in 1941 whose job it was to keep an eye on the Japanese community. Ringle reported that over 90 percent of the Nisei and 75 percent of the Issei were completely loyal to the United States.

"Enemy Aliens"

Not willing to take any chances, FBI agents began their own roundup of three thousand suspected "enemy aliens" just hours after the bombing of Pearl Harbor. About half of those arrested were people of German and Italian descent, individuals who by their ancestry,

behavior, and associations were judged hostile toward the United States. World War II had been raging in Europe for two years, with America's allies, Britain and France, pitted against Hitler's Germany and Mussolini's Italy.

The rest of the suspects were Japanese. Often without warning, wives and children came home to the disturbing discovery that a loved one had been taken for questioning, as Yoshiko Uchida describes:

> When I got home, the house was filled with an uneasy quiet. A strange man sat in our living room and my father was gone. The FBI had come to pick him up, as they had dozens of other Japanese men. . . . In spite of her own anxiety, Mama in her usual thoughtful way was serving tea to the FBI agent. . . . I couldn't share [her] gracious attitude toward him. Papa was gone, and his abrupt custody into the hands of the FBI seemed an ominous portent [sign] of worse things to come.[25]

An FBI agent searches the home of Japanese Americans to ascertain whether they are "enemy aliens" and thereby pose a threat to U.S. security.

Uchida's father worked for a Japanese import-export firm, reason enough to make the FBI suspicious of him. Many of the men arrested were chosen simply because of their occupations—heads of Japanese organizations; executives of Japanese businesses, shipping lines, and banks; and Japanese language teachers and journalists. Some suspects had expressed views that were pro-Japanese, but others were merely community leaders. Some pastors and Sunday school teachers were included. So were commercial fishermen, who were in a position to make contact with enemy ships.

Those men who were judged a threat to their country were taken to special internment camps overseen by the Justice Department, located in North Dakota and Nebraska. There they remained, sometimes for many months. Eventually, those who proved innocent were allowed to rejoin their families, most of whom had meanwhile been sent to relocation camps.

With the arrests, the FBI was satisfied that danger from internal treachery was all but eliminated. Members of anti-Japanese organizations, however, were not convinced that the FBI had done enough to ensure the safety of the West Coast. They began calling for the removal of all Japanese Americans. Groups who competed economically with Japanese Americans also added their voices. "We're charged with wanting to get rid of the Japs for selfish reasons," stated a spokesperson for the Grower-Shipper Vegetable Association in California. "We might as well be honest. We do." [26]

"Yellow Journalism"

The "yellow journalism" press, which thrived on rumors and unverified speculation, was also busy stirring up public fears. Journalists whose job it was to be unbiased often expressed opinions that were one-sided and unfair. Derogatory terms such as "Japs," "Nips," "yellow men," and "yellow vermin" were used interchangeably when referring to Japanese and Japanese Americans. Unfounded articles with titles such as "Jap Boat Flashes Messages Ashore" and "Map Reveals Jap Menace" appeared in California newspapers.

A banner announcing "I am an American" stretches across the front of Wanto grocery store. The Japanese American store owner posted the sign the day after the Pearl Harbor attack to proclaim his patriotism.

General John DeWitt, head of the army's Western Defense Command, believed Japanese Americans living on the West Coast threatened national security during World War II.

Not even the Nisei, who were citizens, were exempt from the accusations. For instance, one journalist for the *Los Angeles Times* wrote, "A viper is nonetheless a viper wherever the egg is hatched—so a Japanese-American, born of Japanese parents—grows up to be a Japanese, not an American." [27] And renowned journalist Edward R. Murrow remarked to a Seattle audience in January 1942 that if Seattle was ever bombed, they "[would] be able to look up and see some University of Washington sweaters on the boys doing the bombing." [28]

Rejected and Threatened

Government and civic leaders were also responsible for whipping up anti-Japanese

feeling through racist remarks and speeches. Members of Congress and senators such as Mississippian John Rankin and Tom Stewart of Tennessee denounced all Japanese and Japanese Americans as cowardly and immoral. In February 1942 the mayor of Los Angeles gave a speech calling for the roundup of all Japanese Americans before they could harm America. Even Earl Warren, later to become California's governor and influential chief justice of the U.S. Supreme Court, stated, "I have come to the conclusion that the Japanese situation as it exists today in this state may well be the Achilles heel of the entire civilian defense effort." [29]

Not surprisingly, such remarks led many ordinary people to react negatively. The reactionaries were a minority of the population; a public opinion poll taken during this period indicated that only 20 to 40 percent of the population supported action against Japanese Americans. Nevertheless, as a result, many Japanese Americans lost their jobs or were forced out of positions they occupied. The Los Angeles County Board of Supervisors fired all its Nisei employees. Officials in Portland, Oregon, revoked the licenses of all Japanese nationals doing business in the city.

Other reactions were more personal. Neighbors made threatening phone calls. Houses were stoned. Japanese passersby were attacked and spat on in the streets. In some places, beatings and lynchings occurred. To prevent mistaken attacks, Chinese Americans began wearing pins that stated "I am a Chinese." Yoshiko Uchida writes, "I wasn't aware of any violence against the Japanese in Berkeley, but there were many reports of terrorism in rural communities, and the parents of one of my classmates in Brawley were shot to death by anti-Japanese fanatics." [30]

One of the most influential government officials to believe the worst about Japanese

Americans was General John DeWitt, in charge of the army's Western Defense Command stationed in San Francisco. DeWitt, a sixty-one-year-old army bureaucrat, was increasingly convinced by every rumor that the United States stood in grave danger from the thousands of Japanese Americans living on the West Coast.

DeWitt conscientiously passed on the "facts" to his superiors. In one memo he wrote that "there were hundreds of reports nightly of signal lights visible from the coast, and of intercepts of unidentified radio transmissions."[31] In another, that "for a period of several weeks following December 7th, substantially every ship leaving a West Coast port was attacked by an enemy submarine. This seemed conclusively to point to the existence of hostile shore-to-ship (submarine) communication."[32]

Most of the information DeWitt chose to believe was exaggerated or untrue. Japanese submarines attacked ships off the California coast extremely rarely and one report existed of a Japanese air attack on oil tanks near Los Angeles, but none of these had involved Japanese Americans. DeWitt's signal lights turned out to be farmers burning piles of brush. "Enemy" radio signals were, in reality, army transmissions. And thousands of guns, ammunition, dynamite, radio receivers, and cameras that had reportedly been confiscated proved to have been gathered from a licensed gun shop and a warehouse. According to Justice Department and FBI reports:

> We have not found a single machine gun, nor have we found any gun in any circumstances indicating that it was to be used in a manner helpful to our enemies. We have not found a single camera which we have reason to believe was for use in espionage.[33]

Man Without a Country

After Pearl Harbor, many West Coast officials feared that Japanese Americans were secretly sending military secrets to Japanese ships and submarines lurking off the Pacific Coast. As a result, Japanese American fishermen—highly suspect because their work took them into coastal waters—were arrested by the FBI, as this incident, recorded in Jeanne Wakatsuki Houston's Farewell to Manzanar, *describes.*

"That night Papa burned the flag he had brought with him from Hiroshima thirty-five years earlier. . . . He burned a lot of papers too, documents, anything that might suggest he still had some connection with Japan. These precautions didn't do him much good. He was not only an alien; he held a commercial fishing license, and in the early days of the war the FBI was picking up all such men, for fear they were somehow making contact with enemy ships off the coast. Papa himself knew it would only be a matter of time.

They got him two weeks later. . . . [T]wo FBI men in fedora hats and trench coats—like out of a thirties movie—knocked on Woody's door, and when they left, Papa was between them. He didn't struggle. There was no point to it. He had become a man without a country. The land of his birth was at war with America; yet after thirty-five years here he was still prevented by law from becoming an American citizen. He was suddenly a man with no rights who looked exactly like the enemy."

On February 19, 1942, President Franklin Roosevelt endorsed Executive Order 9066, authorizing the relocation of all persons of Japanese ancestry.

In fact, there never was a proven case of shore-to-ship signaling or any other sabotage or fifth column activity by Japanese Americans on the West Coast.

To the President

General DeWitt ignored these truths and earlier reports by Munson and Ringle and continued to express his belief that Japanese Americans should be removed from the West Coast. Eventually, his arguments for relocation reached Secretary of War Henry L. Stimson. Stimson was aware of the strong anti-Japanese feeling in California, and he supported the establishment of zones around military installations, oil fields, dams, airports, and other sensitive operations from which Japanese Americans could be excluded. Still, he was reluctant to take the drastic and complicated step of relocating over a hundred thousand people if it was not necessary.

Then, on February 14, 1942, DeWitt sent Stimson a recommendation entitled "Evacuation of Japanese and Other Subversive Persons from the Pacific Coast." The report, and DeWitt's odd logic, apparently helped convince the war secretary of the military necessity for relocation:

> [A]long the vital Pacific coast over 112,000 potential enemies, of Japanese extraction, are at large today. There are indications that these are organized and ready for concerted action at a favorable opportunity. The very fact that no sabotage has taken place to date is a disturbing and confirming indication that such action will be taken.[34]

DeWitt's rationale was extremely weak; he based his argument that sabotage would take place on the fact that it had not yet occurred. After meeting with several War Department officials who also favored internment, however, Stimson went to President Roosevelt to urge relocation.

Earlier, Roosevelt had cautioned his country to guard against discrimination aimed at innocent citizens. However, when Stimson presented DeWitt's recommendations and requested that the president authorize the army to relocate all persons of Japanese lineage as well as others who might threaten the security of the country, Roosevelt agreed. On February 19, 1942, ten weeks after Pearl Harbor, he signed Executive Order 9066.

The German Threat

As war raged in Europe in 1942, German submarines invaded the waters off the East Coast of the United States, torpedoing American ships and taking hundreds of American lives. Despite this threat, the government's treatment of German Americans was significantly different from that meted out to Japanese Americans, as the Commission on Wartime Relocation notes in its report, Personal Justice Denied.

"[The] destructive struggle, with its suggestions of active aid from people on shore, produced no mass exclusion of German aliens or German American citizens from the East Coast. The Justice Department interned East Coast German aliens it thought dangerous, and a small number of German American citizens were individually excluded from coastal areas after review of their personal records. . . .

In the spring of 1942 the War Department seriously considered whether the power of Executive Order 9066 should be used to exclude from certain areas all German and Italian aliens or at least some categories of such enemy aliens . . . [but] the mass movement of Germans and Italians was effectively opposed. With about one million German and Italian aliens in the country, it was quickly recognized that moving such a large group *en masse* presented enormous practical difficulties and economic dislocation. . . . In addition, to have detained many Germans who were already refugees from the Nazis would have been bitterly ironic.

But most critical was the public and political perception of the lesser danger presented by Germans and Italians. . . . No effective, organized anti-German and anti-Italian agitation aroused the public as it had against the ethnic Japanese on the West Coast, and the War Department . . . was not sufficiently persuaded to press the President to allow it."

The order made no mention of any particular race, but it was directed at Japanese Americans. Relatively few persons of German and Italian descent were incarcerated, even though the United States was now also at war with Germany and Italy. Officials argued that German and Italian loyalty was easily determined, while that of Japanese Americans was not.

Although some of his advisers viewed the decision for relocation as extreme and without precedent, the president reasoned that in times of war and for reasons of national security such bold steps often had to be taken. Attorney General Francis Biddle, who opposed the order, later observed:

I do not think [Roosevelt] was much concerned with the gravity or implications of his step. . . . What must be done to defend the country must be done. . . . The military might be wrong. But they were fighting the war. Public opinion was on their side. . . . Nor do I think that constitutional difficulty plagued him—the Constitution has never greatly bothered any wartime President.[35]

Voluntary Relocation

On March 2, DeWitt announced the designation of Military Areas 1 and 2 and warned that, in the near future, certain people might be excluded from those regions. Military Area 1 covered the western halves of Washington, Oregon, and California and the southern half of Arizona. Military Area 2 included the rest of these states.

Relocation had already begun, however, with a call for volunteers. As early as December 1941, Japanese Americans patriotic (or fearful) enough to disrupt their lives and leave their communities had been asked by Justice Department officials to move out of certain sensitive areas around military installations.

The result was chaos and confusion. Rumors of internment camps and mandatory evacuation were rampant; families asked themselves if they should go or stay and risk imprisonment. Jeanne Wakatsuki Houston, whose father had been arrested by the FBI, writes, "I remember my brothers sitting around the table talking very intently about what we were going to do, how we would keep the family together."[36] Most families who decided to cooperate were faced with trying to dispose of their property and possessions in a short period of time, usually at a huge monetary loss.

Decisions had to be made about where to go, how to get there, and how to make a living on arrival. Some families decided to make

Japanese Americans voluntarily register for evacuation from Seattle on March 10, 1942.

Hatred and Fear

As Japanese Americans left the West Coast in response to the government's call for voluntary relocation, citizens in neighboring states proved to be no less prejudiced than those in the West. An example of this irrational hate and fear can be found in a letter sent to the governor of Utah in 1942, and published in Japanese Americans: From Relocation to Redress.

"We will not tolerate Japanese here to sabotage and blast our industries, water systems, defense plants, and beautiful cities. . . .

How can we afford to enlist our own good American boys, whom we have raised for purposes other than war, to fight Japanese aggression and at the same time allow these people to roam at will within our country? . . .

Governor, I hope you will keep these ruthless barbarians, these plague-dispensing savages far removed from our homes and farms and industries. We have fifty-six Japs living in our town limits and others are coming. Fourteen percent of our school children are Japs and the Japanese children tell our youngsters that they will show them who is boss as soon as those California kids get here. If we must have these Japs in our communities, let's have them in camps and under strict supervision."

A Nisei family inspects their home after neighbors scrawled anti-Japanese graffiti on the walls.

the move as short as possible. For instance, many from Los Angeles relocated to Fresno. (In June 1942, DeWitt declared all California a prohibited zone, so these families had to move again.) Many decided to move to neighboring states, such as Nevada and Idaho. The most daring—usually Nisei with excellent language skills—went farther east, either to try and make a life for themselves on their own or to join the rare family member who had left the Pacific Coast.

"Japs Keep Moving"

Not surprisingly, people living in such states as Idaho and Wyoming believed that their dams, airports, and military installations were just as vulnerable to sabotage as were those in Pacific states. Almost as prejudiced as Californians, many were outraged by the influx of Japanese Americans who arrived from the West Coast expecting to resettle.

Refugees were met with hostility and with signs like "Japs Keep Moving. This is a White Man's Neighborhood." Some were turned back at state borders by armed and angry men; some were thrown in jail. Community leaders worried that mob violence was imminent.

By the end of March, over three thousand Japanese Americans had cooperated with the government, but nearly one hundred thousand still remained in Military Areas 1 and 2. Those numbers, coupled with increasing tension throughout the West, forced DeWitt to declare voluntary relocation a failure. Now the move would be compulsory. In a new policy outlined in late March, the general announced that all persons of Japanese lineage were to be evacuated from Military Area 1 in the near future. This included not only full-blooded Japanese, but anyone who had

Japanese blood, "no matter how small the quantum." A number of Koreans, Hispanics, and Blacks, married to Japanese, chose not to be separated from their spouses and children; they were relocated, as well.

Canada and Hawaii

The United States was not the only country to take such forcible steps against its Japanese American population. Feelings against the Japanese ran high throughout North, Central, and South America during the course of the war. In cooperation with the U.S. State Department, a few Latin American countries sent Japanese citizens living in their nations to U.S. internment camps, from which they were later used as bargaining chips in diplomatic exchanges with Japan. In Alaska and Canada, the entire West Coast Japanese population was relocated to camps in a move similar to that in the United States.

Ironically, the U.S. territory of Hawaii, deep in the war zone, did not imprison most of its Japanese both because Hawaiians were more racially tolerant and because Japanese made up a large percentage of its workforce. Locking them up would have had a devastating effect on the local economy. Thus, most were allowed to remain in their homes and jobs for the course of the war.

"Why Us?"

The evacuation announcement was no surprise to the Japanese American community, but all were hurt and humiliated by the decision. They had done nothing to warrant such unfair treatment. As former internee Emi Somekawa asked, "Why us? I felt like we were just being punished for nothing." [37]

Members of the Japanese American Citizens League (JACL) post instructions in both English and Japanese to help prepare Japanese residents of Seattle for evacuation. The league strongly urged its members to cooperate with the authorities.

Despite these feelings, leaders of the JACL, one of the few organizations to represent Japanese Americans, urged cooperation with authorities. "You are being removed only to protect you and because there might be one of you who would be dangerous to the United States. It is your contribution to the war effort. You should be glad to make the sacrifice to prove your loyalty."[38]

Many Japanese, particularly the Nisei, were critical of the JACL's compliant stance. They accepted the fact that the Issei, who were Japanese citizens, might justly be incarcerated as enemy aliens in times of war. But imprisoning American citizens threatened the constitutional freedoms of all Americans. Jack Tono remembers, "I just couldn't under-

stand the whole atmosphere of the whole thing, being a citizen. I could see it if I was an alien. You have no choice but to face things like that. But at the JACL meeting when . . . nobody resisted . . . it was more shocking than the goddarn Pearl Harbor attack. It really frosted me."[39]

Veterans of World War I were equally outraged. They felt betrayed by the country for which they had fought and despised anyone who cooperated with the government. One veteran, Joe Kurihara, believed that all should fight against relocation "to the bitter end." "These boys claiming to be the leaders of the Nisei were a bunch of spineless Americans," he declared, referring to the JACL. And regarding the government: "Having had absolute confidence in Democracy, I could not believe my very eyes what I had seen that day. America, the standard bearer of Democracy, had committed the most heinous crime in its history."[40]

Other Nisei argued that uprooting hundreds of loyal and peaceable persons to remove a few potentially dangerous individuals from the West Coast was unnecessary and unjust. And to the government's argument that relocation was for their own good, to protect them from public violence, another Nisei pointed out, "The government could have easily declared Martial Law to protect us."[41]

Despite their criticism, few Japanese Americans actively resisted relocation. Prior to the Executive Order, some had signed petitions and attended meetings at which they begged their country to act fairly. Once

the order was signed, however, their traditions and upbringing led them to obey authority. They had no leaders who encouraged their defiance. Thus, most expressed their disillusionment privately or not at all.

To some Japanese Americans the order to relocate came as something of a relief. Since Pearl Harbor they had lived with uncertainty. Many Issei had had their bank accounts frozen and had lived in poverty for months. Some believed that deportation to Japan was just around the corner; others feared violence. "[T]o be unable to go out in the streets, or just to the corner store without the fear of being insulted," remembers one evacuee, "and being all tense inside with that same fear, was one of the most humiliating things."[42]

Thus the notion of going into a camp, away from a hostile and threatening world,

Japanese evacuees follow an army escort to trains that will transport them to a relocation center. Meanwhile friends and relatives, many of whom will also be evacuated, crowd the overpass to bid them farewell.

seemed to some like a step toward stability. The camps would provide shelter, food, and protection. There everyone would be of Japanese lineage. As that same evacuee admitted, "I think some of us were a little relieved to be away from the minor irritations, the insults, slander, and the small humiliations unthinking people heaped upon us after Pearl Harbor."[43]

Model Citizens

The great majority of Japanese Americans on the West Coast were model citizens, as Jack Tono observes:

> [T]here was no ethnic group as strait-laced as the Japanese because of their historical background. . . . [W]e're all brought up with honor, shame, dignity; the moral code of standards is nothing but the best. When you talk about delinquency and other crime, for us there was nothing but traffic tickets.[44]

In fact, many people recognized the community's good qualities and deplored the injustice of the relocation decision. They pledged continued support of their Japanese American neighbors and colleagues. They urged unity and cooperation between races. Some expressed their views by letter to President Roosevelt. One asked, "Do you think the President . . . could find it suitable and wise, at a press conference or even in a fireside talk, to say a word of praise for the American citizens of Japanese descent, loyal and of good record, who . . . have endured and are enduring no little hardship?"[45] Another wrote, "Has the [government] really

Most Japanese Americans proved to be model citizens and won the support of their white neighbors and colleagues.

power to intern American citizens? Is it reasonable for Japanese-Americans to be interned and Germans and Italians, not? Is not the very essence of our democracy that we are made up of all races and colors?"[46]

As events continued to unfold, however, even the most concerned had to face the fact that the government was not going to consider or protect Japanese American rights. All the evacuees could do was make the best of their situation—by proving their loyalty to America, by following government directives, and by packing up their families and moving into the unknown. "We took whatever we could carry," one Nisei recalled later. "So much we left behind, but the most valuable thing I lost was my freedom."[47]

Protective Custody

I f the weeks after the bombing of Pearl Harbor were difficult for Japanese Americans, the days leading up to relocation were a nightmare. The government tried to disguise the fact that it was sending them into prison camps by using euphemisms such as "non-aliens," "protective custody," and "reception centers."

Reality was different, however. Beginning in late March 1942 and continuing throughout the summer, terse commands called Civilian Exclusion Orders appeared on telephone poles and shop windows in Japanese communities, directing all persons to prepare to move within the week. Those who did not comply faced severe penalties including arrest and imprisonment. Those who obeyed reported to a Civil Control station in their community, where they were registered and given a number by which they would be known during internment. One recalls, "I lost my identity. . . . The WRA [War Relocation Authority] gave me an I.D. number. That was my identification. I lost my privacy and dignity." [48]

An Agonizing Process

Preparing to move was an agonizing process. Families were directed to bring only a minimum of belongings to camp, but were responsible for their own clothing, eating utensils, towels, and bedding—blankets and sheets. Most also packed tea kettles, hot

**WESTERN DEFENSE COMMAND AND FOURTH ARMY
WARTIME CIVIL CONTROL ADMINISTRATION**
Presidio of San Francisco, California
April 1, 1942

INSTRUCTIONS
TO ALL PERSONS OF
JAPANESE
ANCESTRY
Living in the Following Area:

All that portion of the City and County of San Francisco, State of California, lying generally west of the north-south line established by Junipero Serra Boulevard, Worchester Avenue, and Nineteenth Avenue, and lying generally north of the east-west line established by California Street, to the intersection of Market Street, and thence on Market Street to San Francisco Bay.

All Japanese persons, both alien and non-alien, will be evacuated from the above designated area by 12:00 o'clock noon Tuesday, April 7, 1942.

No Japanese person will be permitted to enter or leave the above described area after 8:00 a. m., Thursday, April 2, 1942, without obtaining special permission from the Provost Marshal at the Civil Control Station located at:

1701 Van Ness Avenue
San Francisco, California

The Civil Control Station is equipped to assist the Japanese population affected by this evacuation in the following ways:

1. Give advice and instructions on the evacuation.
2. Provide services with respect to the management, leasing, sale, storage or other disposition of most kinds of property including: real estate, business and professional equipment, buildings, household goods, boats, automobiles, livestock, etc.
3. Provide temporary residence elsewhere for all Japanese in family groups.
4. Transport persons and a limited amount of clothing and equipment to their new residence, as specified below.

The Following Instructions Must Be Observed:

1. A responsible member of each family, preferably the head of the family, or the person in whose name most of the property is held, and each individual living alone, will report to the Civil Control Station to receive further instructions. This must be done between 8:00 a. m. and 5:00 p. m., Thursday, April 2, 1942, or between 8:00 a. m. and 5:00 p.m., Friday, April 3, 1942.

2. Evacuees must carry with them on departure for the Reception Center, the following property:
    (a) Bedding and linens (no mattress) for each member of the family;
    (b) Toilet articles for each member of the family;
    (c) Extra clothing for each member of the family;
    (d) Sufficient knives, forks, spoons, plates, bowls and cups for each member of the family;
    (e) Essential personal effects for each member of the family.

All items carried will be securely packaged, tied and plainly marked with the name of the owner and numbered in accordance with instructions received at the Civil Control Station.

The size and number of packages is limited to that which can be carried by the individual or family group.

No contraband items as described in paragraph 6, Public Proclamation No. 3, Headquarters Western Defense Command and Fourth Army, dated March 24, 1942, will be carried.

3. The United States Government through its agencies will provide for the storage at the sole risk of the owner of the more substantial household items, such as iceboxes, washing machines, pianos and other heavy furniture. Cooking utensils and other small items will be accepted if crated, packed and plainly marked with the name and address of the owner. Only one name and address will be used by a given family.

4. Each family, and individual living alone, will be furnished transportation to the Reception Center. Private means of transportation will not be utilized. All instructions pertaining to the movement will be obtained at the Civil Control Station.

Go to the Civil Control Station at 1701 Van Ness Avenue, San Francisco, California, between 8:00 a. m. and 5:00 p. m., Thursday, April 2, 1942, or between 8:00 a. m. and 5:00 p.m., Friday, April 3, 1942, to receive further instructions.

J. I. DeWITT
Lieutenant General, U. S. Army
Commanding

SEE CIVILIAN EXCLUSION ORDER NO. 5

A facsimile of the Civilian Exclusion Orders that were posted in San Francisco on April 1, 1942. The notice gives detailed instructions on evacuation procedures and is signed by General John DeWitt. Japanese residents of San Francisco were given only one week to get their affairs in order and evacuate the city.

A *Japanese American business owner hangs a poster advertising an evacuation sale. Without someone to oversee operations, evacuees were forced to sell their businesses—usually at a considerable loss.*

plates, books, and other small, personal items. Yoshiko Uchida writes:

> In one corner of my mother's room there was an enormous shapeless canvas blanket bag which we called our "camp bundle." Into its flexible and obliging depths we tossed anything that wouldn't fit into the two suitcases we each planned to take. We had been instructed to take only what we could carry, so from time to time we would have a practice run, trying to see if we could walk while carrying two full suitcases.[49]

Unsure of their final destination, adults worried about packing appropriate clothes for their families. If they went to the mountains, winter clothing would be a necessity. In warmer climates, heavy sweaters and coats would only take up valuable space. One woman remembers, "They said 'camp,' so we thought about going up in the mountains somewhere. I even bought boots thinking we would be up in the mountains where there might be snakes. Just ridiculous all the funny things we thought about."[50]

Adults also worried about disposing of household goods they could not take along. Most people were not wealthy, but the majority had a car or truck and a houseful of furniture. Each family member also had his or her own prized possessions—porcelain tea sets, houseplants, trunks of family mementos and heirlooms—most of which had to be left behind.

Finding homes for family pets was another difficult task. Families sometimes left their animals with friends. Others resorted to giving pets away. Yoshiko Uchida recalls the fate of the family dog. "Although the new owner of our pet had promised faithfully to write us in camp, we never heard from him. When, finally, we had a friend investigate for us, we learned . . . that Laddie had died only a few weeks after we left Berkeley."[51]

Storage and Sales

Since taking everything to camp was not an option, most families sold some of their more valuable household items, usually at a small fraction of their value. The *Los Angeles Times* wrote that "junkmen and second-hand furniture dealers" were preying on many who were desperate for money. Nearly new washing machines sold for $5; refrigerators for $10. Rather than sell her family furniture for a few dollars, one woman made a bonfire and burned everything. Another who had been offered $17 for a set of china worth over $300, smashed her delicate cups and saucers in front of the dealer who had made the offer.

Businesses and homes were also sold at a loss by families who had no one to act as caretaker. One woman observed, "We sold the store for a thousand dollars the day before we left. We had done an inventory, and the contents of the store were worth ten thousand. Our machines alone were worth eight thousand—that's what we paid for them. And we sold the whole store for a thousand dollars."[52]

But not every American was out to take advantage of the Japanese community. Many generous people offered to oversee homes and farms that had to be abandoned, and to store boxes of possessions that could not be taken to camp. Yoshiko Uchida remembers, "We were close to our neighbors and they both extended the warmth of their friendship to us in those hectic days. We left our piano and a few pieces of furniture with one, and we piled all the miscellaneous objects that remained on the last day into the garage of the other."[53]

E-Day

In late March, nervous but obedient Japanese Americans began reporting to the control centers on their assigned evacuation day (known as E-Day). As they gathered, dozens of volunteers, many from neighboring churches, helped them cope with children, suitcases, boxes, and bags. Some volunteers handed out coffee, tea, and doughnuts, so that no one would begin the trip on an empty stomach. In San Francisco, the Quakers set up a canteen offering, besides the usual refreshments, hot plates to heat baby bottles, string to tie up boxes, and tissues for those who could not hold back their tears. Many volunteers went so far as to drive the sick and aged to assembly centers so they would not have to cope with a difficult train or bus ride.

On E-Day in April 1942, a Japanese American girl peers through the wooden slats of a truck bed while waiting to evacuate San Pedro, California, for an assembly center.

Strange Migration

Up and down the West Coast, evacuation day marked the beginning of internment for all Japanese American communities. Exhausted and despairing, evacuees nevertheless did their best to hide their feelings and comply with the rules. Yoshiko Uchida describes her E-Day experience in Desert Exile.

"It wasn't until I saw the armed guards standing at each doorway, their bayonets mounted and ready, that I realized the full horror of the situation. Then my knees sagged, my stomach began to churn, and I very nearly lost my breakfast.

Hundreds of Japanese Americans were crowded into the great hall of the church and the sound of their voices pressed close around me. Old people sat quietly, waiting with patience and resignation for whatever was to come. Mothers tried to comfort crying infants, young children ran about the room, and some teenagers tried to put up a brave front by making a social opportunity of the occasion. The women of the church were serving tea and sandwiches, but very few of us had any inclination to eat.

Before long, we were told to board the buses that lined the street outside, and the people living nearby came out of their houses to watch the beginning of our strange migration. Most of them probably watched with curious and morbid fascination, some perhaps even with a little sadness. But many may have been relieved and glad to see us go."

Japanese Americans are met by armed guards upon their arrival at the Santa Anita Assembly Center in California on April 4, 1942.

A young evacuee sits with her family's belongings while waiting to board a train bound for an assembly center.

Once the journey into the unknown began, however, the atmosphere became less friendly. Stark signs of mistrust were all around. Armed guards were ever present. In some rail cars, windows had been papered over to prevent passengers from looking out. Former internee Miyo Senzaki remembers, "We got on, and as we traveled, I noticed that wherever we hit a town, the MPs [military police] would tell us to pull the shades down and we'd be curious, because we didn't know where we were going."[54]

Resistance and Despair

Most Japanese Americans cooperated when it came to relocating, but some tried to evade the move. One Nisei went into hiding and was found, near starvation, three weeks later. Fred Korematsu, a young Californian who eventually challenged the constitutionality of evacuation in court, underwent plastic surgery and successfully posed as a Spanish-Hawaiian for a time until he was arrested by the FBI.

For a few, the relocation process was too humiliating to be borne. Rather than shame himself and his daughter, a father afflicted with a medical condition that would have been revealed in the public atmosphere of the camps committed suicide. A World War I veteran did the same, dying with his Honorary Citizenship Certificate in his hand. The certificate had been awarded in "honor and respect for your loyal and splendid service to the country in the Great World War."[55]

Assembly Centers

Once begun, the process of relocation was so rapid that few permanent relocation centers had been built before internees began arriving at control stations, suitcases in hand. Until the centers were completed, therefore, most families were sent to one of twelve temporary reception centers, officially known as assembly centers. Manzanar and Poston Relocation Centers were the exceptions; both were close to completion, so some evacuees went directly into them from their homes.

Army officials in charge of this phase of relocation chose existing facilities such as racetracks and fairgrounds as sites for the assembly centers, since these public places had been designed to hold large numbers of people and were already equipped with electricity, water, and bathroom facilities. The addition of barbed wire and armed guards around the perimeters ensured that residents would not try to escape.

Within the centers, grandstands, livestock stalls, and stables were turned into apartments for the residents. The rooms were drafty and cold during bad weather and oppressively hot on sunny days. Dividing walls were paper thin and sometimes did not reach the ceiling. The floors of many stalls were only scraped out and covered with boards, so that, in the summer heat, the smell was overpowering. As Yoshiko Uchida describes,

> The stall was about ten by twenty feet and empty except for three folded Army cots lying on the floor. Dust, dirt, and wood shavings covered the linoleum that had been laid over manure-covered boards, the smell of horses hung in the air, and the whitened corpses of many insects still clung to the hastily white-washed walls.[56]

Other residents were housed in hastily built barracks—shacks with tar paper roofs—dubbed "chicken coops" because of their low ceilings and lack of windows. A bare light-bulb hung from the ceiling, and furniture consisted of army cots and mattress tickings that had to be stuffed with straw before they could be used. On arrival, stunned residents could do little but unpack their meager possessions and wonder how long they would be forced to live in such conditions.

A Lasting Impression

Living quarters were not the only disheartening and demeaning features of camp life. On rainy days, walkways turned into ankle-deep mud as thousands of residents tramped from

Newly arrived internees crowd between rows of makeshift apartments at the fairgrounds in Stockton, California. Army officials converted racetracks and fairgrounds into temporary assembly centers to facilitate relocation.

Makeshift Accommodations

During the early days of internment, internees were crowded into makeshift accommodations at racetracks and fairgrounds until more permanent relocation camps were completed. In The Kikuchi Diary, *edited by John Modell, internee Charles Kikuchi describes quarters under the grandstands at the Tanforan Race Track near San Francisco.*

"The Grandstand is almost filled with single men and it probably is the most interesting place in camp. There are about 500 men in there and when they all take their shoes off, the odor that greets you is terrific. What a stench! . . . But the place is a study of varied activities. In one corner a sullen Kibei has built himself a little cube so that he can work on his master's thesis. Just down the aisle from him, an old Issei has set up a home made barber shop and he is doing a brisk business. . . . Little knots of Japanesy [pro-Japan] men cluster around the radios blaring the latest news and discussing the final Japanese victory. A brave Nisei occasionally opens his mouth and he is shouted down. But three American flags continue to hang upon the walls. Other single men sprawl out in their beds, smoking or playing Japanese cards. A few sleep with their mouths wide open, snoring like mad, which adds to the general confusion. Over in the far corner, there is a lone but seedy looking minister with a dirty collar, who sits so straight in his bed reading a Buddhist prayer book. Flies buzz around him, but he pays no attention."

apartments to mess halls and back again. Plumbing in laundries and bathrooms periodically backed up due to overuse. Conditions in the mess halls were unappetizing and unsanitary, and hundreds of residents suffered from food poisoning because food was incorrectly stored and handled. Former internee Minoru Yasui remembers his experiences in the Portland assembly center, where many families lived in the livestock pavilion.

My lasting impression of the dining area was that it was festooned with yellowish, spiral flypaper hung from posts and rafters. Within a short time the paper would be black with flies caught in the sticky mess. There were horseflies, manure flies, big flies, little flies, flies of all kinds. . . . Flies, after all, usually inhabited livestock barns.[57]

The Takemoto family sits at the entrance to Apartment 3, their meager living quarters in Manzanar Relocation Center. Residents of the centers nicknamed these tar paper shacks "chicken coops" because of their appearance.

Bad Taste

Hastily organized camp routines did not run smoothly during the early days of internment. Lines were an ever-present fact of life. Little attention was paid to the internees' preferences and tastes, as Jeanne Wakatsuki Houston describes in Farewell to Manzanar.

"We had pulled up just in time for dinner. The mess halls weren't completed yet. An outdoor chow line snaked around a half-finished building that broke a good part of the wind. They issued us army mess kits, the round metal kind that fold over, and plopped in scoops of canned Vienna sausage, canned string beans, steamed rice that had been cooked too long, and on top of the rice a serving of canned apricots. The Caucasian servers were thinking that the fruit poured over rice would make a good dessert. Among the Japanese, of course, rice is never eaten with sweet foods, only with salty or savory foods. Few of us could eat such a mixture. But at this point no one dared protest. It would have been impolite. I was horrified when I saw the apricot syrup seeping through my little mound of rice. I opened my mouth to complain. My mother jabbed me in the back to keep quiet. We moved on through the line and joined the others squatting in the lee of half-raised walls, dabbing courteously at what was, for almost everyone there, an inedible concoction."

Nonexistent Privacy

With thousands of people crowded into each assembly center, residents immediately discovered that every moment of the day was shared. Families were constantly thrown together in their tiny one-room apartments. Neighbors were so close that even the smallest sounds were detectable. Minoru Yasui remembers, "Because of the thinness of the three-ply wood, any noise—any coughing or sneezing, crying of babies, family arguments, boisterous conduct, laughing, or any shouting or yelling—could be heard throughout the hall."[58]

Meals were communal. Three times a day, residents carried their eating utensils to noisy mess halls, where lines were long, food was served cafeteria style, and everyone ate at crowded picnic tables.

Bathrooms and showers were also communal, and this was one of the most disturbing discoveries. Older Japanese, who habitually finished their day with the private luxury of a hot, relaxing bath, now found themselves compelled to shower shoulder-to-shoulder with strangers in an open room intended for horses. Women were horrified at the sight of rows of toilets, ranging back-to-back down the middle of the room. As one remembers, "For us women . . . it was just a shock. I remember we got sick . . . we couldn't go . . . we didn't want to go. . . . It was very humiliating."[59]

Some tried to solve the problem by carrying newspapers, behind which they could at least hide their faces and pretend to read. Some chose to use the bathrooms in the dead of night; others erected portable cardboard partitions around themselves. Eventually, carpenters constructed wooden partitions (without doors) around each toilet, but, as Yoshiko Uchida observes, "To say that we all became intimately acquainted would be an understatement."[60]

Relocation

There were many aspects of the centers that challenged the residents who were used to the privacy and comfort of their own homes. Yet, with persistence and creativity, most soon began to adjust to their new surroundings. They made new friends, settled into their apartments, and established new routines. Just as they did so, however, center officials made a disturbing announcement. Construction of the relocation centers was nearly complete. Barracks had been erected, water supplies developed, sewage systems built, and power lines strung. Internees would soon be transferred into them, and the assembly centers would close.

The news created fresh anxiety and added to the uncertainty of everyone's already unsettled lives. They had already given up their homes and property and begun anew. Now they were being told to repack their few possessions and begin all over again. They wondered when they would be leaving, what the permanent centers would be like, and if they would remain together as families. Charles Kikuchi wrote in his diary: "The suspense of getting our order [to move] is getting me down. I know that it is coming soon, but when? I hope that they will give us two or three days of advance notice so that we can pack." [61]

Notice was accordingly given, and between June and the end of October 1942, residents were transferred to one of ten relocation camps, located on federally owned land and run by the War Relocation Authority (WRA), an agency established by President Roosevelt for that purpose.

Dusty and Desolate

The relocation centers were located in desolate regions of the country, far from towns, highways, and railroads, since many Americans

Internees at Poston Relocation Center dine in a spartan mess hall in this 1943 photograph.

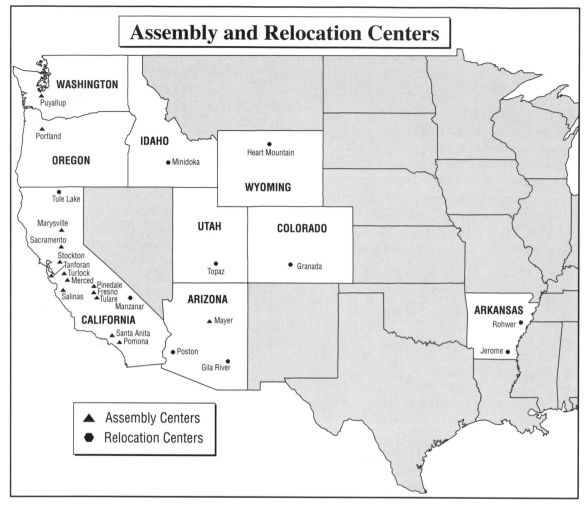

Assembly and Relocation Centers

WASHINGTON
▲ Puyallup

▲ Portland

OREGON

IDAHO

● Minidoka

Heart Mountain ●

WYOMING

● Tule Lake

Marysville ▲

Sacramento ▲

Stockton ▲
▲ Tanforan
▲ Turlock
▲ Merced
▲ Pinedale
▲ Fresno
Salinas ▲ ▲ Tulare
Manzanar ●

CALIFORNIA

UTAH

COLORADO

● Topaz

● Granada

ARIZONA

▲ Mayer

● Poston

Gila River ●

Santa Anita ▲
▲ Pomona

ARKANSAS

Rohwer ●

Jerome ●

▲ Assembly Centers
⬢ Relocation Centers

rebelled at the thought of treacherous "foreigners" living near them. Jerome and Rohwer camps were built on Arkansas swampland infested with malarial mosquitoes. Poston's three wards, or blocks of barracks, known as Poston, Toastin', and Roastin', were set in the sun-scorched Arizona desert. Topaz center was located in a barren Utah valley and recorded temperatures that ranged from 106°F in the summer to below freezing in winter. Manzanar, located in the dry Owens Valley in eastern California, also experienced similar temperature extremes. Jeanne Wakatsuki Houston, who lived in Manzanar, writes,

"Some old men left Los Angeles wearing Hawaiian shirts and Panama hats and stepped off the bus at an altitude of 4000 feet, with nothing available but sagebrush and tarpaper to stop the April winds pouring down off the back side of the Sierras."[62]

Residents at Manzanar, Topaz, Minidoka, and Heart Mountain also suffered through dust storms, clouds of swirling grit that regularly turned day into night and shut down all activity for hours at a time. Even in calm weather, dust constantly filtered up through cracks in barrack floorboards, defying all efforts to sweep it away. One former Manzanar resident remembers, "The desert was bad enough. . . . The constant . . . storms loaded with sand and dust made it worse. . . . Down in our hearts we cried and cursed this government every time when we were showered with dust. We slept in the dust; we breathed the dust; and we ate the dust."[63]

Towns Surrounded by Barbed Wire

The relocation centers were not brutal concentration camps like those established in Nazi Germany for the Jews, but they were prisons nevertheless, surrounded by barbed wire fences, guard towers with machine guns, and searchlights. Wards were arranged side by side with military precision. In a typical center, there were nine wards—four blocks per ward, sixteen to twenty-four barracks per block.

Each block had a kitchen, mess hall, laundry, bathrooms, and showers. Empty barracks were used as meeting halls, recreation rooms, churches, and schools. The centers were also equipped with a hospital, fire station, staff houses, and storage warehouses. Acreage within center boundaries was usually cultivated and crops were used to feed the residents.

The barracks themselves, usually partitioned into six apartments, were flimsy structures made of boards and covered with black tar paper. Each apartment was about twenty by twenty feet, the size of a small living room. None had running water. Heat was provided by an oil-burning stove, and furniture consisted of one army cot and two blankets per person. An average family was usually assigned to one apartment; couples and single persons were sometimes made to share an apartment, and larger families were allotted two.

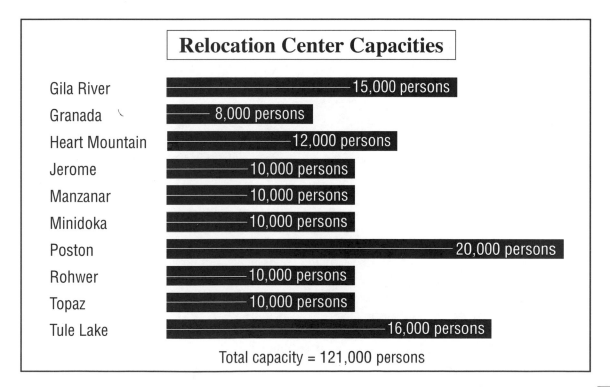

Relocation Center Capacities

Gila River	15,000 persons
Granada	8,000 persons
Heart Mountain	12,000 persons
Jerome	10,000 persons
Manzanar	10,000 persons
Minidoka	10,000 persons
Poston	20,000 persons
Rohwer	10,000 persons
Topaz	10,000 persons
Tule Lake	16,000 persons

Total capacity = 121,000 persons

(Below) The American flag flies above dusty Manzanar relocation camp. (Right) At Poston, located in the scorching Arizona desert, new residents stuff mattresses with straw.

Improvements

In dozens of irritating ways, internees were reminded that they were little better than criminals, but they soon realized that life in the camps was an improvement over the months spent in the assembly centers. Privacy was still at a premium—apartments were cramped and bathrooms and laundries were communal—but most of the camps covered thousands of acres, so now there was space for residents to walk around outside. Jeanne Wakatsuki Houston remembers, "[I]t was an

out-of-doors life, where you only went 'home' at night, when you finally had to: 10,000 people on an endless promenade inside the square mile of barbed wire that was the wall around our city."[64]

Barracks were poorly built, with cracks in the floorboards and walls that allowed icy wind and sand inside, but they were an improvement from stables and "chicken coops," and residents soon made them more homelike. Within weeks, curtains hung at most windows, lids of tin cans covered knotholes in the walls, and homemade furniture, vases of flowers, and throw pillows brightened the stark rooms. After a time, sheetrock and linoleum—maroon, black, and forest green—were installed in most barracks, making them more weatherproof and more attractive.

Food was again served cafeteria style in mess halls, but its quality gradually improved, especially after residents began growing their own vegetables and raising poultry. From the beginning, as in the assembly centers, meals were "American" and included such items as hot dogs and hamburgers, which pleased members of the younger generation. Charles

Kikuchi wrote in his diary, "There can no longer be conflict over the types of food served, everybody eats the same thing, with forks."[65] In time, fish, rice, and other foods preferred by older Japanese were added to menus in most centers.

Controlled and Supervised

Despite these improvements, internees never forgot that their every move was controlled and supervised. Each camp had a director, appointed by the national director of the War Relocation Authority, first Milton Eisenhower and later Dillon Myer. A few directors were men who lacked the tact and understanding needed for dealing with the complexities of camp life. For instance, Ray Best, head of Tule Lake Relocation Center, allowed radical nationalist internees to dominate and intimidate innocent Tule Lake residents for months.

Most directors, however, were responsible, businesslike individuals who tried to cope fairly in the midst of difficult situations. Ralph Merritt, head of Manzanar, often went out of his way to aid residents. Paul Robertson of the Leupp Isolation Center (a high security facility for troublemakers) treated his prisoners with respect and even corresponded with several after internment ended.

Each director had a staff who helped run the camp. In the beginning, all were Caucasian. As time passed, however, Japanese Americans proved ready and able to take over many assistant positions and do most of the work in offices and mess halls. There were Caucasians on the staff who were bigoted and unhelpful, but overall the group was dedicated and hardworking, saw the internees as equals, and treated them with understanding

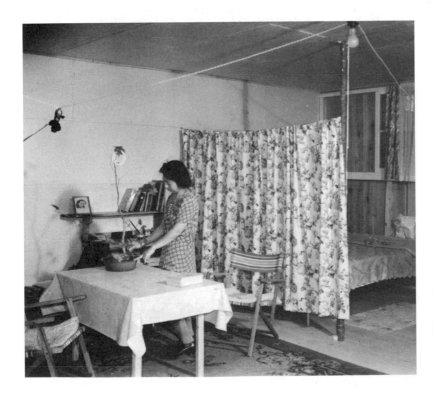

Curtains, rugs, and furniture made from scrap lumber help to improve and personalize this typical apartment in Jerome Relocation Center in Arkansas.

Protective Custody **49**

and tolerance. One internee testified to his supervisor's kindness: "He did not like to have me say that I was working for him, for he said we were working together for the good of 10,000 people. We worked night and day, but I did not mind, for I was working with a man who could not have been finer."[66]

A Constant Presence

Army soldiers who served as guards and sentries were a constant presence in every center. Since internees showed little or no desire to escape (at Topaz, internees themselves erected the fences and towers after they arrived), a minimum detail of officers and enlisted men was assigned to each camp. During times of disturbances, more soldiers were brought in.

Guarding the centers was boring duty for those who were away from their families and had little to do during the long months they served. Charles Kikuchi observed in his diary, "Sort of feel sorry for the soldiers. They are not supposed to talk to us, but they do. Most are nice kids. They can't get leaves and so have nothing to do."[67]

Kikuchi was more accepting of his captors than most of the internees. To them, the guards represented the army and the government, which all now hesitated to trust. And while some guards were sympathetic, others were not. As one WRA official reported, "[Lt. Buchner] explained that the guards were finding guard service very monotonous, and that nothing would suit them better than to have a little excitement, such as shooting a Jap."[68] In fact, in several incidents, guards wounded and even killed internees, one of

The Howling Wind

Built in dry and desolate settings, camps such as Manzanar and Topaz were subject to terrific dust storms that swept in at a moment's notice and lasted for hours. In her book Desert Exile, *Yoshiko Uchida describes her terror when she is caught in one such storm.*

"If I thought the dust I had breathed and absorbed so far was bad, I had seen nothing yet. About a week after we arrived, I encountered my first dust storm. . . . I happened to be in another block walking home with a friend when the wind suddenly gathered ominous strength. It swept around us in great thrusting gusts, flinging swirling masses of sand in the air and engulfing us in a thick cloud that eclipsed barracks only ten feet away.

My friend grabbed my hand and pulled me into the nearest laundry barrack, but even inside, the air was thick with dust. The flimsy structure shuddered violently with each blast of wind, and we could hear garbage cans and wooden crates being swept from the ground and slammed against the building. We waited more than an hour, silent and rigid with fear, but the storm didn't let up. I was afraid the laundry barrack might simply break apart and the howling wind would fling us out into the desert, but I was too terrified even to voice my thoughts. When at last the wind wasn't quite so shrill, we decided to run for our home barracks so we wouldn't be trapped where we were until night."

Army sentries stand guard in the watchtower at Santa Anita. A strong military presence existed in both the assembly and relocation centers.

whom had only carelessly wandered too close to a perimeter fence. Thus, it is not surprising that the sentries' attempts to be friendly were politely ignored by most internees.

High Security Camps

While most center residents were law abiding and required a minimum security presence, certain internees came to be seen as troublemakers and were sent to special camps where they could be more carefully guarded.

One of the highest security facilities for such troublemakers was located in Moab, Utah. Overseen by the WRA, this camp was populated by Nisei from mainstream camps who had been judged guilty of crimes ranging from organizing work stoppages, strikes, and protests, to having pictures of Japanese soldiers pinned in their apartments. In some cases of mistaken identification, innocent internees were held and given no chance to return to their families even when the mistake was discovered.

Life at Moab was grim; administrators there paid little attention to the comfort or preferences of the prisoners. Rules were strict; guards were ordered to shoot to kill; and the most dangerous men were under constant guard, even in showers and bathrooms. Predictably, internee morale was low, as one inmate's words reveal: "The life here has been worse than a prisoner's life. . . . In the event that our internment will be until after the war, there may be much bitter disillusionment brewing from this cruel camp life."[69]

In April 1943, WRA authorities closed Moab and transferred its inmates to a similar camp in Arizona. Located on a desolate Navaho reservation, Leupp Isolation Center proved to be an improvement over Moab, thanks to its humane director, Paul Robertson. Under Robertson, camp conditions were no worse than in mainstream centers, and prisoners were given greater freedom than they had experienced at Moab. Leupp was closed in December 1943 when its fifty-two inmates were transferred to Tule Lake camp, which became the new center for disloyal citizens.

Justice Department Camps

Moab and Leupp held Japanese American citizens; certain Issei identified as dangerous "enemy aliens" were incarcerated instead in camps operated by the Justice Department, located in Santa Fe, New Mexico; Bismarck, North Dakota; Missoula, Montana; and Crystal City, Texas. Almost all internees in these camps were men—generally older—who were suspected by the FBI of having ties with Japan. A large number were Japanese who had been transferred from Central and South America. Some were diplomats. Also interned were those individuals of German and Italian descent who had been judged a threat by the FBI early in the war.

Although under high security, internees in these camps lived similarly to internees in WRA relocation camps. All were housed in barracks, provided with an adequate diet, and allowed to develop recreation, education, and work programs. Their greatest single concern was for their families, from which they were often separated for years. Inmates at Crystal City Center were spared this hardship, since women and children were allowed to voluntarily join husbands and fathers, but, as one historian writes, "for the majority of the internees, there would be no family reunion for the duration, and no relief from this anguish."[70]

Patient Endurance

Whether internees lived in mainstream relocation camps or high security centers, every aspect of their lives was colored by the fact that they were not free. The fact that they had been suspected and presumed guilty by their government and their fellow Americans was not easily overlooked or forgotten.

However, most had been taught to bear hardship patiently, to put their personal feelings aside, and to work for the common good. They had endured prejudice and discrimination before the war. Now they were ready to do all they could to make the best of their days, even though the future appeared difficult and uncertain.

Creating Communities

Despite the harsh living conditions and uncertainty of their days, the internees wasted no time in bringing order and meaning to their lives. From the beginning, many worked tirelessly to establish and maintain important organizations and institutions—school, church, government, etc.—of society at large. So successful were they, and so well did they adapt to their new world, that some almost forgot they were surrounded by barbed wire and armed guards. Others discovered, to their surprise, unexpected advantages in their new lifestyle.

Newfound Leisure

Issei women, in particular, noticed a change for the better upon entering the centers. Their former lives had consisted of unending hard work—cleaning, shopping, cooking, sewing, etc. They had reared children. When necessary, they had worked in the fields or helped run businesses with their husbands. Few had had leisure time to sit and talk with friends.

Now all that changed. Single-room apartments required little cleaning, and meals came fully prepared three times a day. Some clothing was provided by the government; utilities were free and there were few bills to be paid. Not only did women have time for friendships, they had time to take care of themselves and to develop new interests and hobbies. One woman, who discovered a tal-

ent for poetry, expressed her appreciation of such leisure time:

> Fortunate me; Indifferent
> To the fierce fighting
> All over the world,
> Here I am, learning
> Flower arrangement, writing, and
> embroidery.[71]

Older men saw their time in camp as a kind of well-earned vacation, as well. They too filled their spare time with activities they had been too busy to pursue before the war. Many passed the time talking and playing games such as poker and *go*, a traditional Japanese board game. Others tried gardening, rock collecting, or carving miniature boats. Charles Kikuchi noted in his diary, "The sailboats of the Issei are getting bigger and better. One old man even has a motor in his. They take a radio down to the lake [at the Tanforan Assembly Center] and play it while sailing the boats all day long."[72]

Teaching by Instinct

Most residents were not content with virtually uninterrupted rest and relaxation, however. One of every four internees was a child, so college-educated Nisei began organizing schools, some of the first institutions to be established in the camps. Classes began in the assembly centers and were led by volunteers, whose purpose it was to bring order

Fourth-graders study colonial history at their school within Poston Relocation Center. Because 25 percent of all internees were children, schools were the first institutions established in the camps.

into the children's lives and help counteract the negative effects of imprisonment. Few Japanese Americans had been allowed to teach in public schools up to this time, so teachers were inexperienced but eager. As Yoshiko Uchida explains, "I taught mostly by instinct. The children, however, were affectionate and devoted."[73]

After the move to relocation centers, the WRA took over these informal attempts at education and hired Caucasian teachers to live and work in the camps. Many were older women who had not taught for several years. Some were missionaries; a few were conscientious objectors performing alternative service in the camps rather than in combat. Under their supervision, students went on to establish school newspapers, athletic clubs, and honor societies. Organizations usually associated with schools—PTAs, Boy Scouts and Girl Scouts—also became a part of camp life.

"A Shortage Beyond Comprehension"

Despite the effort and good intentions, relocation center schools had many shortcomings. Since classrooms were flimsy and open to the elements, windstorms, blizzards, and heavy rain often shut down classes. Space was at a premium and educators were scarce due to the war, so classes were overcrowded. One teacher might supervise fifty students. To make matters more difficult, several classes were often jammed together in unpartitioned meeting and dining halls, and the clatter of silverware and dishes distracted students and teachers. Charles Kikuchi observed, "The school is a vast hubbub of voices—some low, some high pitched. . . . Above this din, the teachers try to compete and they have to speak very loudly in order to get themselves heard."[74]

Perhaps the most difficult obstacle to overcome was the lack of supplies. Students and teachers alike were dismayed on first entering schoolrooms that were completely bare. For a time, classes met with no desks, tables, chairs, blackboards, books, or pencils. High school students, trying to prepare for college, lacked other necessities. Former internee John Kanda remembers, "There was absolutely no equipment— especially for laboratory courses—and there was really a shortage beyond comprehension of textbooks."[75]

Even faced with such obstacles, most Japanese American students eagerly went to class and studied hard. Thousands persevered through high school and graduated while in camp, then went on to a college or professional school. For others, however, the stress, uncertainty, and deprivations of camp life eventually took their toll and they lost their enthusiasm for learning. Cheating, disrespectful attitudes, bullying, and vandalism, which had seldom troubled the Japanese American community before, reached problem levels. One teen wrote, "My life's ambi-

tion was to be a nurse, and though I think of it often yet, I'm afraid, very much afraid that I will be unable to carry out my plans. . . . I have lost interest in school and . . . my desire for a nursing career has lessened."[76]

Expressions of Faith

Along with education, residents also relied on churches, Christian and Buddhist, to provide structure and spiritual support in their lives. In their efforts to fit into American society, a great many Japanese immigrants (originally Buddhists) had converted to Christianity and were rearing their children as Christians. Methodists were the largest Protestant group represented, but there were members of all other denominations, as well as Catholics, Mormons, and Quakers. In many centers, a nondenominational "Christian" church was set up to prevent rivalry and discord. Buddhist leaders followed the same practice. In general, the majority of Buddhists were Issei.

For Christians, Sunday services in the camps were of the traditional variety with

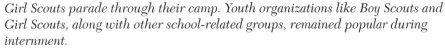

Girl Scouts parade through their camp. Youth organizations like Boy Scouts and Girl Scouts, along with other school-related groups, remained popular during internment.

Sunday schools for children and midweek prayer services for the most devout. Riici Satow, a Baptist, had hardly settled into his living quarters before he became involved in church activities. "We had morning service and evening service on Sunday, an officers' meeting on Monday, a prayer meeting on Wednesday and . . . there was another one, which I can't recall now. Anyhow, we had five meetings a week. Our new church was in full swing from then on." [77]

Church was not only a symbol of faith for many residents, but an important link to the outside world. Missionaries regularly visited the centers and attracted large crowds. Churches were also sites for the many weddings and funerals that took place in every center. Yoshiko Uchida remembers, "One of the elementary school teachers was the first to be married at Tanforan. She . . . wore a beautiful white marquisette gown with a fingertip veil. . . . After a reception in one of the recreation centers, [she and her husband] began their life in one of the horse stalls." [78]

Concerned Outsiders

Visitors were another link to the outside, and did much to normalize life for residents through encouragement and the many goods they provided. At some centers, such as Tanforan, a racetrack near San Francisco, so many visitors arrived on weekends that center officials had difficulty keeping track of everyone. (Reportedly, a man who owned property across from the racetrack opened a parking lot there on Sunday afternoons and made a tidy profit by charging a fee of fifteen cents a car.)

Churches located within the camps allowed internees to practice their religion. Here, a resident of Heart Mountain in Wyoming stands beside the altar of the camp's Buddhist church.

Internees and War Relocation Authority (WRA) officials worked together to establish schools in all the camps. The quality of education, however, could not be compared to that offered on the outside, as internee John Kanda explains in And Justice for All.

"We were sent to Tule Lake in September, and school started late, sometime after we arrived.... The teachers that taught grade school or high school were just volunteer people who had some experience in the line of whatever course they were asked to teach. So I'd have to say they were far inferior to other teachers in the state.... There were no textbooks to take home or even to borrow to take home, and there weren't enough even to be distributed one to each pupil during the class hour. Whatever you had almost always had to be shared, and this was my senior year in a college preparatory course.... I finished the chemistry course in high school at Tule, but when I went to college I knew zero.... I never saw a Bunsen burner or a beaker or a flask until I got to college.... I think they [the teachers] tried hard, but the equipment wasn't there, and the school was in a barracks. They had a blackboard and chalk and that was about it."

Many visitors were friends from internees' former churches and neighborhoods. Others were professors from the colleges and universities Japanese American students had attended. Yoshiko Uchida writes:

Our own visitors included not only my father's business associates, but our neighbors, my piano teacher ... and many church and university people we had known over the years.... They came because they were our friends, but also because they were vitally concerned over the incarceration of one group of American citizens on the basis of race, and the denial of our constitutional rights.[79]

Members of the Society of Friends, known as Quakers, were some of the most dedicated visitors to the centers, regularly bringing warm clothes, household supplies, and home-cooked meals. Their presence also helped to improve conditions in the centers, as author and former internee Michi Nishiura Weglyn explains: "The patience of the Army authorities was ... sorely tried by the presence of these busy, ubiquitous Quakers, who were quick to criticize, as in their condemnation of the stables and shacks as out-and-out fire traps."[80]

Ironically, the American Civil Liberties Union (ACLU), ordinarily outspoken advocates of those whose civil rights are threatened or violated, made little protest against the injustice of internment. Instead, the national office took the position that the decision to relocate Japanese Americans was well within the government's rights, since the nation was at war. In defiance of national policy, the ACLU's Northern California branch supported the internees' cause, particularly after serious physical abuse occurred at Tule Lake camp in 1944.

Councils and Controversy

Self-government was another aspect of center life designed to increase organization and

Members of the community council at Manzanar meet to discuss camp issues. Council members helped to maintain peace in the camps and mediated between administration and internees.

stability. In the first months of internment, the WRA announced that elected community councils would be allowed to act as spokespersons and liaisons between internees and staff, with the goal of encouraging the smooth running of the centers.

Campaigns for the position of community council member sparked enormous interest among the internees. Candidates printed and distributed flyers and made speeches. Charles Kikuchi observed, "The political campaigns for the camp elections are going full blast ahead now. . . . The YD's [Young Democrats] are well organized and have a good chance. . . . Posters are plastered all over the place. Somebody even got the bright idea of putting posters in the toilet bowls."[81]

Unfortunately, support for the councils weakened after the WRA stipulated that no Issei could run for office. The rationale was reasonable. Issei were not citizens; many of

them did not speak English well; a small number were outspokenly pro-Japanese. The ban, however, created many factions in the camps. Some internees supported the system in spite of the ban. Others believed that council members—usually young adult Nisei—were only "administration stooges." As one former internee writes, "Most blocks at first had at least a few outspoken men or women who were vigorously anti-administration in attitude. In block meetings they urged resistance to . . . most things that the administration wanted done."[82]

Committee members often found themselves in the awkward position of relaying administration policy to rebellious internees and trying to win concessions from the administration in order to maintain camp harmony. Still, many councils did manage to function and successfully deal with such matters as juvenile guidance, recreation, food quality, public relations, and education.

Jobs for Low Pay

Politics did not appeal to the majority of internees, so many residents turned to work to fill the long days in camp. No internee was required to work, but all who did received salaries for their labor. Unfortunately, the pay was so low—between eight and sixteen dollars a month, compared with Caucasians in the camps who earned ten times as much—that camp employment might as well have been classified as volunteer labor.

Some residents took on such mundane tasks as sorting and delivering mail, operating boiler rooms, and doing office work for the administration. Others served as cooks and dishwashers, unexpectedly stressful jobs when that meant serving three meals a day to hundreds of people. Charles Kikuchi wrote, "I saw one Issei dishwasher slap a Nisei girl because she complained that the cups were so dirty. Their nerves are on edge in the cooking division because they are the target for many complaints."[83]

Some internees set up small businesses such as repair shops and beauty parlors. Some organized and operated dry goods stores that sold essentials and notions such as thread and needles, moth balls, shoe polish, and soap. In Manzanar, many Nisei worked making camouflage nets that were used in the war.

Farms in the Desert

Agriculture was a part of every center, and many farmers took great pride in the crops they produced, despite the harsh conditions and barren land on which they worked. Manzanar workers cultivated about fifteen hundred

Newsletters to Newcomers

Every camp had its own newspaper, published several times a month by a Japanese American staff. Contents were approved by camp administrators, and ranged from advertisements and personal columns to international and local news. William Hosokawa, a University of Washington graduate formerly interned at Heart Mountain Relocation Center in Wyoming, reports the origins of one such paper in And Justice for All.

"It was necessary to get information out to the residents. Very soon they were coming into the camp at the rate of five hundred to six hundred every two or three days . . . and they had to be assigned barracks and mess halls, and it was essential to get out information to these people. So we began to issue a series of bulletins—newsletters to the newcomers—telling them about the camp, what the regulations were, giving them a little background. That was the start of the information program. Eventually we started a weekly newspaper, the Heart Mountain *Sentinel*. I became editor of the paper, and I enjoyed that kind of work, as much as one can enjoy anything working behind barbed wire. . . .

I should point out that there was no overt 'censorship' of what we were doing. There was a certain amount of staff censorship. But we tried to be very objective in the way we covered the news, and we tried to confine our opinions to the editorials of the paper, and these were generally supportive of the government program."

Residents of Manzanar converted nearly fifteen hundred acres of barren land into productive farmland. This photograph, taken by renowned photographer Ansel Adams, shows a typical day on the Manzanar farm.

acres; Gila River camp in Arizona planted over seven thousand. Crops included a wide range of vegetables including cabbage, squash, and tomatoes, as well as field crops such as soybeans and guayule, from which rubber could be extracted to be used in the war. At Manzanar, untended orchards abandoned by previous landowners were revived, and soon thousands of boxes of apples and pears were available for internees living there.

Internees were also allowed to raise beef cattle, poultry, and hogs, and many of the camps were self-sufficient for meat as well as food crops. Some centers also became involved in food processing. For instance, tofu-making plants were a part of each camp, and Manzanar processed all its own soy sauce.

Clinics in Horse Barns

From the earliest days of relocation, Japanese American doctors, nurses, and dentists offered their services to the internees, regularly delivering babies, immunizing children, treating victims of food poisoning, and giving care and support to the old and infirm. All professionals in the centers worked under conditions that would have horrified most doctors and nurses on the outside. Fred Fujikawa, a doctor interned at Jerome Relocation Center in Arkansas, describes conditions he observed at the Santa Anita Assembly Center.

The hospital at Santa Anita looked like a shed which I understand was used for saddling the horses. . . . We had a clinic at one end, and we had patients at the other end. . . . We had the general hospital to back us up so we were pretty confident. However, there were only six of us taking care of some eighteen thousand inmates there.[84]

For the most part, facilities in the relocation centers were more permanent and hygienic than in assembly centers. And patients suffering the most serious illnesses and injuries were transported to city hospitals where they were treated by specialists. But, as Emi Somekawa, a nurse at the Tule Lake center remembers, "There were a lot of unnecessary deaths in camp. You wouldn't

A dentist attends to a patient in his clinic at Minidoka Relocation Center in Idaho.

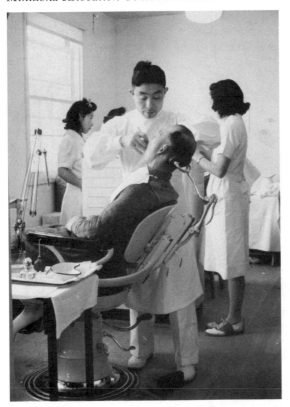

believe it. It's just that there were not enough people to watch the patients, not enough professionals. It's just that kind of thing."[85]

The Lighter Side

While churches, schools, and politics provided much needed structure and stability for residents, life in the centers was not without its lighter side. Holidays were celebrated with baseball games and parades on the Fourth of July and decorated trees and gift exchanges at Christmas. Sports of all kinds were popular, and internees constructed running tracks, tennis courts, swimming pools, and small golf courses at many centers. Playground swings and slides were purchased and installed for small children. In some centers, streams were dammed to form lakes where families enjoyed passing an evening with their children or couples strolled along pathways lined with newly transplanted trees.

Those internees who enjoyed gardening took great pride in making their barren surroundings as beautiful as possible. Some worked together to create large gardens and landscaped parks that required constant care. One internee remembered the Gila River Relocation Center, set in the Arizona desert, as having been converted into a beautiful community with lawns, trees, and vegetable gardens. Another described the "mossy nooks, ponds, waterfalls and curved wooden bridges"[86] that were part of a park in Manzanar.

For internees who preferred indoor pastimes, libraries provided a variety of reading material. (Books were donated by friends and sympathetic organizations.) Theatrical companies put on productions complete with sets and elaborate costumes, ordered from the outside. Musicians formed bands and orchestras

All-American Sport

Baseball, that all-American sport, was a popular pastime for many internees. Every camp had a number of enthusiastic teams—boy and girl—and players were sometimes allowed short-term leave to play against outside teams, as Page Smith relates in Democracy on Trial.

"The pride of Minidoka (which preferred to call itself Hunt after the local Post Office), was its high school baseball team. When the center team played the Twin Falls High School team at Minidoka, the Minidoka team won by a score of 16 to 4 while some four thousand enthusiastic evacuees (almost half the population of the center) cheered their team on. The next night the Minidoka team played before a large crowd in Twin Falls and the result was the same, a 16 to 4 Minidoka victory. The beat went on. The Filer High School team was Hunt's next victim. Having defeated seven high school teams from nearby towns, the Hunt team traveled 175 miles to Idaho Falls to play in the state championship. There they were beaten by a team whose pitcher, it was said, had recently pitched for the New York Yankees, a ringer. The Hunt team claimed that a third of the spectators cheered them on. Perhaps the sweetest victory was at home against the military police team from the center. With the score 14 to 1, the game was called as no contest."

Crowds of internees gather to watch a baseball game at the Tule Lake camp.

Young internees enjoy a night of dancing in their high school's auditorium at Poston in 1944.

and performed everything from classical music to the jitterbug for high school dances. Classes offered instruction in ceramics, tap dancing, singing, and flower arranging, and craft lovers created unique objects such as decorative mailboxes and elaborately carved walking sticks. Occasionally, movies were shown in the mess halls, although watching them was an uncomfortable experience. Charles Kikuchi noted, "Seeing a show is a form of self-torture. One sits on the floor and the cushions do not eliminate the hardness of the boards. . . . About halfway through the picture, your neck gets awfully stiff from looking up at an angle."[87]

Quality of Life

Many parents worked hard to provide the quality of life their children had enjoyed before internment. For instance, internee June Toshiyuki often took her young ones, and others from her block, on walks to the cattle yards where the youngsters could climb the haystacks. She remembers, "If they saw a canal, the boys would jump in and swim. We had so much fun together."[88] Other parents worked to provide that quality in a different way. Just as before the war they had sacrificed and saved and encouraged their children to go to college, now they did the same, hoping that those who showed an interest in higher education would be allowed to leave the camps.

Education was only one of several routes that young internees took to get out of the centers. For many, their release occurred because the country needed their services, both at home and abroad. As Michi Weglyn writes, "Needs now outweighed prejudices, forcing open for the internees the sought-for wedge for an escape, a much earlier one than the Army had intended."[89]

Outside the Wire

Most Japanese Americans longed for the day internment would end. Thomas Takeuchi, a former internee at Minidoka Relocation Center in Idaho, says, "We were in the darkness while at the center, constantly dreaming of the day when the sun would come out of the dark overhanging clouds to shine on [us] and we would be allowed to be free."[90]

Despite their dreams, few internees defied authority and tried to escape from the camps. Most friends and family members lived in the next barracks or were behind the wire in other centers. Outside, society was openly hostile to everyone with Asian features. Thus, escapes were rare and usually involved extenuating circumstances. Two instances had to do with individuals who were mentally or emotionally ill. Another involved a young man who was under suspicion of murder. In perhaps the most innocent instance, thirty-two children faced arrest for sneaking out of Heart Mountain Relocation Center in Wyoming in order to go sledding on a nearby snowy hill.

Exceptional cases aside, internees usually left the camps only with permission. They clung to the belief that by cooperating with authorities they would convince everyone of their trustworthiness.

Short-Term Leave

Although willing to follow the rules, internees took advantage of every opportunity to get out of the centers. And after the Battle of Midway in June 1942 ended the threat of Japanese attack on the United States, WRA officials began permitting some internees to temporarily leave camp for various reasons. Schoolchildren and their teachers were allowed to take field trips into the surrounding countryside. High school baseball teams visited other schools for league play. Certain individuals were granted short-term leave to visit family members in other centers. Yoshiko Uchida remembers one trip taken by her parents. "It cheered my father enormously to see his mother and sister. . . . But more than that, it was the trip itself, enabling my parents to live freely outside the barbed wire enclosure even for a brief period, that had renewed their spirits."[91]

Students Go East

Many young Japanese Americans were able to resettle out of the camps by pursuing a higher education. At the time of Pearl Harbor, almost twenty-five hundred Nisei were attending colleges and universities on the West Coast. Educators such as Robert Gordon Sproul, president of the University of California, and Lee Paul Sieg, president of the University of Washington, were quick to express concern that internment would interrupt the education of these young people who were loyal supporters of the United States. Church leaders also wrote letters to

Smoke billows from an American aircraft carrier during the decisive Battle of Midway. The U.S. victory ended the possibility of a Japanese invasion.

President Roosevelt, suggesting that colleges and universities in the East consider the possibility of enrolling young Japanese Americans who wanted a higher education.

By the summer of 1942, the National Japanese American Student Relocation Council had been formed, with branches located on both the East and West Coasts. Initially, the council worked to resettle college students from western to eastern schools, but eventually it became involved in college placement for high school seniors in the camps. Scholarships from concerned Protestant groups helped fund this higher education, as did money raised by internees.

For instance, at Topaz in Utah, residents raised almost $200,000 in donations to help college-bound students achieve their goals.

Unexpected Opportunity

Many large colleges and universities in the East had defense contracts or were located near prohibited facilities such as defense installations and railroad tracks. Since these institutions could not or would not accept the Nisei, students usually enrolled in small, private schools, which they found to be friendly and accepting. One student wrote, "Already I have met some of the finest acquaintances I have known. Although there are only two [Japanese Americans] here, we are not lonesome, as the Caucasians are more friendly." Another observed, "The professors actually get to know you, they say hello to you by your right name! . . . It took a considerable time to accustom myself to all this."[92]

Admittedly, there were some setbacks in the student resettlement program. For instance, in the fall of 1942 the University of Idaho rejected six students because of racial tension on its campus. But by the summer of 1944 the relocation council had successfully placed thousands of students, many of whom had graduated from high school in the camps, in colleges and universities across the country. This resettlement enabled many young Japanese Americans to reach new heights in their chosen careers. One student working in the East wrote, "Hundreds . . . are employed in occupations which were denied to them on the Pacific Coast."[93]

Industrious and Intelligent

Applying for "work leave" was another popular way that Japanese Americans could gain clearance to leave the centers. By the summer of 1942, thousands of Caucasian farm laborers had gone to war. Farmers, especially sugar beet growers in the West, were desperate for laborers to work in the fields. An agreement was soon reached whereby Japanese Americans could be released temporarily in order to harvest beets and other crops. Volunteers from among an initial pool of almost two thousand willing men and women were transported to farms and paid a minimal wage (less than two dollars a day) for long hours of grueling physical labor. But, as Yoshiko Uchida remembers, "A call for sugar

beet workers on outside farms was immediately filled, because there were any number of men who wanted to escape the confusion and disarray of life inside the barbed wire."[94]

Volunteers for work outside the camps were required to pass stringent security checks. Once outside, many faced discrimination and harassment. Living conditions were often no better than inside the centers. For instance, one former internee recalls, "Our living quarters was a shack without running water, heated by a coal stove, and we had to bathe in a ditch." Sometimes conditions were worse. "When we arrived there, we were met by a farmer supervisor who led us to a large horse barn, one third of which was filled with hay," another internee testified. "He told us this was where we were going to sleep."[95] Still, most endured the hardships for the sake of freedom, and by 1943 the value of the Japanese American labor force had been recognized. More men and their families were granted "indefinite leave," which meant they could work outside the camps for longer periods if they found work and a place to live.

Urban Settlers

More than nine thousand internees—usually Nisei who spoke English well—went out to work in agriculture-related jobs during the course of the war. They were later recognized as some of the most intelligent and hardworking laborers who ever worked in that industry. From mid-1942 on, many individuals and their families were also encouraged to resettle in urban communities in the East, far from the prohibited zones they could not reenter. They were aided by the WRA, which set up resettlement offices throughout the country. WRA officials also enlisted the help

Agricultural Leave

The agricultural leave program, organized by the War Relocation Authority in the summer of 1942, was seen by many young internees as a means of escaping the camps. Some, however, were ill prepared for the grueling conditions they had to endure, as Paul Shinoda, a college graduate with a wife and three children, describes in And Justice for All.

"We ended up in Blackfoot, Idaho, and they lined us up. And the farmer got to choose us. . . . It was traumatic, lining us up like slaves at the market. They did everything but open your mouth and look at your teeth and feel your muscles. . . .

I was a farmhand and cut hay . . . and that was a lousy job. You had to cut the hay with a horse. I never drove a horse before in my life, and when you go around the corner you've got to raise the bar. It was a wonder I didn't fall off that . . . thing; and if you did, it would have cut your legs off. . . . Parker [the owner] worked hard too, and then after that, it got to be grain harvest time. . . . We helped in threshing, and that was a tough job. It hurt my back permanently.

Then came potato harvest. Jack Parker would take the tractor and dig the potatoes and lay them on top of the ground with the machine. Then the guys on piecework would pick them up and put them in gunnysacks of about sixty-five or seventy pounds. Dusty, dirty, and heavy work, and I got ninety dollars a month, and the ones picking the potatoes were making fifty dollars or twenty dollars a day."

A farm labor shortage during the war forced farmers to recruit Japanese American internees to help harvest their crops.

After obtaining "work leave" permits, these Japanese Americans left Rohwer camp in Arkansas and relocated to Wisconsin to work in the fields.

of community leaders and other interested groups to reduce prejudice and help the settlers fit into their new communities.

Of course, some internees had mixed feelings about leaving the camps. Jobo Nakamura, a resident of Tule Lake, wrote:

> Life here has made me soft and indolent. I'm clothed, sheltered, and I don't have to worry about where my next meal is coming from. . . . I must go out and make my living the hard way again. Yet doubt and fear disturb my mind. Would I be jumping out of a frying pan into the fire? Will I be happy outside in a strange community? To go out means to depart from

my lifelong friends. It means to tear myself away from a life of comparative ease and security to start life all over again. It makes me feel weary.[96]

Early groups of settlers, however, paved the way for family and friends who dared to follow. Soon, groups of Japanese Americans were scattered throughout the United States. Some worked on farms, some in factories, and some in professional positions. One woman, Helen Kitaji, taught Indian children near the small town of Window Rock, Arizona. Another, Haruko Niwa, became a director of a resettlement association in Milwaukee, Wisconsin.

Life in a Japanese American Internment Camp

Secret Weapons

Among the most admired Japanese Americans to resettle out of the camps were those young men who joined the U.S. military and fought in the war.

Even before internment, many Nisei had assumed that they would be allowed to fight for their country. But when they tried to enlist, they discovered that the government did not want them. Japanese American soldiers, already in the military, were being discharged. Hopeful recruits were listed as 4-F, physically or mentally unfit for service, or 4-C, a status reserved for enemy aliens.

As months passed, however, the government's attitude changed toward Japanese American enlistment. The military needed all the soldiers it could get. In particular, it needed Japanese-speaking individuals to translate captured Japanese documents and monitor radio traffic in the Pacific. Ironically, most Nisei volunteers had only a rudimentary knowledge of Japanese, but they willingly attended Military Intelligence Specialist School to learn the language, then went on to become "secret weapons" for the United States. Without publicity or fanfare they provided valuable skills that helped speed up the Allied victory in the Pacific.

For Their Country

Not only did the government need intelligence specialists, it needed ordinary foot soldiers, as well. In February 1943, President Roosevelt approved a plan that would allow young Nisei males to sign up for combat duty in Europe. One year later, Secretary of War Stimson reinstituted the draft for all qualified Japanese Americans.

By December 1944, over fifteen hundred young Japanese American men had been drafted from the centers. (Women also participated in the war effort. Although none saw combat, hundreds served in the WACs, as army nurses, and in the Red Cross.) Most

Controversial Issues

Although many Nisei dreamed of fighting for their country, military service and the draft were controversial issues for others, such as Tom Watanabe, an internee at Manzanar Relocation Center in California, whose reaction to requests for volunteers appears in And Justice for All.

"They had the guy from the 100th Battalion where the 442nd [all-Nisei Combat Team] came down to camp and asked for volunteers. And at that particular time I had already been in camp six months. So when they told us that they wanted Niseis to volunteer, well, I told them I'd go providing they'd let me go out and live like a human being for six months, and if the government wanted to draft me I'd go like anybody else, because everybody else isn't jumping on the bandwagon and volunteering. All of them are waiting to get drafted. They're working in the aircraft plant and making money. They're waiting to get drafted, so I'll do the same thing. I'll go out and live, but don't touch me for six months. Let me live like a human, and then if you want to draft me I'll go. So they kept me in camp. That was my answer to the draft volunteer."

joined the 442nd Regimental Combat Team, an all-Nisei unit that, together with the 100th Infantry Battalion, made up of Hawaiian-born Japanese, saw action in North Africa, Italy, and France. Many strongly objected to serving in a segregated unit, but Tom Kawaguichi, a member, gives his reasons for joining:

> In the 442nd, a lot of us felt that this was our only chance to demonstrate our loyalty; we would never get a second chance—this was it. We saw the treatment that we were getting and we wanted there to be no question about what we were and where we were going. At least that's the way I felt: give me a chance, at least, to show what I can do or can't do.[97]

"Go for Broke"

The 442nd took as its motto "Go for Broke." Future senator Daniel Inouye, a member of the unit, explained its meaning: "To give everything we did, everything we had; to jab every bayonet dummy as though it were a living, breathing Nazi; to scramble over an obstacle course as though our lives depended on it; to march quick-time until we were ready to drop, and then to break into a trot."[98]

Distinguished by its valiant efforts, the 442nd became the most decorated unit in the army and received numerous awards for bravery. The courage and determination of the Nisei troops eventually helped convince most Americans of Japanese American patri-

Members of the 100th Infantry Battalion, a segregated unit composed of Japanese Hawaiians, march through Italy in 1944.

During a rainy ceremony at the White House, President Harry Truman presents the Distinguished Unit Citation to the 442nd Regimental Combat Team.

otism. As President Harry Truman said when he presented the Distinguished Unit Citation to the 442nd in 1946, "You fought not only the enemy but you fought prejudice and you have won."[99]

The Changing Character of the Centers

As more young, educated, and Americanized Nisei resettled, the character of the centers changed. A large portion of those remaining were elderly, pro-Japanese, or nervous about moving East into unfamiliar areas. Some balked at doing anything the government suggested, no matter how beneficial that might be. One internee said, "Even the very mention of the word 'relocation' makes residents resentful and makes some bristle with resentment."[100]

Resentment characterized an increasing number of residents as time passed. Internees had lived for months in an atmosphere of rumor, suspicion, and distrust. For all they knew, something worse than internment waited for them just around the corner. Troubled and pessimistic, they clung to what they had and waited for the next blow to fall.

Reaction to Betrayal

Young and old, male and female, almost every Japanese American felt deeply betrayed by the action their government had taken against them. As time passed, reaction to that betrayal was expressed both in troubled relations between families and friends and in dramatic and far-reaching upheavals that sometimes swept the camps and left permanent scars. Only a few individuals took a stand and legally protested the violation of their constitutional rights. As Miyo Senzaki, a former internee, explains, "If our leaders at the time were mature and knew the answers and had the wisdom, if there were enough of those people, then maybe things would've been different. There weren't. You can just count on your hands the Nisei who tried to oppose it."[101]

This mother of three had trouble holding back her tears on E-Day. Most Japanese Americans felt betrayed by the U.S. government; once relocated, these feelings caused squabbles among families and friends.

Deliberate Defiance

Few Japanese Americans challenged the legality of the government's action against them in the spring of 1942. Ironically, Minoru Yasui, who chose to protest by deliberately defying his curfew, had difficulty getting the attention of the authorities, as he describes in John Tateishi's And Justice for All.

"On March 28, 1942, I began to walk the streets of Portland, up and down Third Avenue until about 11:00 P.M., and I was getting tired of walking. I stopped a Portland police officer, and I showed him a copy of Military Proclamation No. 3, prohibiting persons of Japanese ancestry from being away from their homes after 8:00 P.M.; and I pulled out my birth certificate to show him that I was a person of Japanese ancestry. When I asked him to arrest me, he replied, 'Run along home, sonny boy, or you'll get in trouble.' So I had to go on down to the Second Avenue police station and argue myself into jail. I pulled this thing on a Saturday and didn't get bailed out until the following Monday.

After being released I called my mother in Hood River. Dad had been interned; she was at home alone with two of her youngest children. Earlier, the Portland *Oregonian* had come out with a front-page, two-inch headline across the top of the page, trumpeting 'Jap Spy Arrested.' I knew that Mom would be worried. I said, 'Mom, *shimpai shiteru dessho?*' ('You are worried aren't you?') I wanted to reassure her that I was physically okay. Her response was, and I shall never forget, 'Shimpai dokoro ka! Susumeru zo!' ('Worry? Nonsense! I encourage you!')"

A Restriction of Personal Liberty

Minoru Yasui, Gordon Hirabayashi, Fred Korematsu, and Mitsuye Endo were four exceptional individuals who dared stand alone and challenge in the courts the government's action against Japanese Americans. Minoru Yasui, a young attorney who had volunteered and been rejected for military service at the beginning of the war, deliberately violated the curfew regulation that existed in his native Portland, Oregon. He explained the reasoning behind his actions:

It was my feeling and belief, then and now, that no military authority has the right to subject any United States citizen to any requirement that does not equally apply to all other U.S. citizens. Moreover, if a citizen believes that the sovereign state is committing an illegal act, it is incumbent upon that citizen to take measures to rectify [correct] such error.[102]

Hirabayashi, a Quaker and a senior at the University of Washington, also deliberately violated the curfew that required all persons of Japanese ancestry to remain in their homes between 8 P.M. and 6 A.M. In addition, he disregarded relocation orders, claiming that the government was violating the Fifth Amendment by restricting the freedom of innocent Japanese American citizens.

Both Yasui and Hirabayashi took their cases to court, lost their suits, and later appealed the decisions to higher courts. Yasui spent several months in prison in Oregon, then was transferred to the Minidoka Relocation Center in Idaho. Hirabayashi's case was eventually heard by the Supreme Court, which in 1943 ruled that a person's rights could be abridged during times of war. Only Justice Frank Murphy, who reluctantly sided with the majority, expressed his reservations. He wrote, "Today is the first time . . . that we have sustained a substantial restriction of the personal liberty of citizens of the United States based on the accident of race or ancestry. . . . It bears a melancholy resemblance to the treatment accorded to [Jews] in Germany."[103]

Legalizing Racism

Fred Korematsu had no intention of taking his case to court when he defied relocation in 1942. A welder in the San Francisco Bay area, Korematsu ignored the order so he could remain near his Caucasian girlfriend. However, he was soon recognized as Japanese by a suspicious drugstore clerk and was arrested and jailed.

While in jail, Korematsu was visited by Ernest Besig, head of the American Civil Liberties Union in northern California. Besig helped Korematsu challenge the constitutionality of relocation, claiming that the government had no right to remove and imprison a group of people solely because of their ancestry. Like Hirabayashi and Yasui, however, Korematsu lost his case, and was sent to Topaz Relocation Center. In December 1944, the Supreme Court upheld his conviction by a 6-to-3 vote, basing their decision on the fact that Korematsu had violated evacuation orders that had been law at that time. Justice Murphy, who expressed the minority opinion, wrote, "Being an obvious racial discrimination, the order deprives all those

within its scope of equal protection of the laws as guaranteed by the Fifth Amendment. . . . I dissent, therefore, from the legalization of racism."[104]

Mitsuye Endo was the fourth challenger of relocation, basing her legal case on the argument that the government had no right to keep *loyal* citizens in prison camps. Endo, a civil servant with a brother serving overseas in the army, obediently followed government orders and went with her parents to Tule Lake center in 1942. Once there, she applied for a writ of habeas corpus—a demand that she be brought to court to decide the legality of her imprisonment. The concept of habeas corpus is a legal safeguard that protects citizens against illegal detention or imprisonment.

Endo waited two and a half years for her case to come before the Supreme Court. When it did, the justices not only decided overwhelmingly in her favor, they declared that "whatever power the War Relocation Authority may have to detain other classes of citizens, it has no authority to (detain) citizens who are . . . loyal."[105]

The Endo case was the landmark that officially ended a bleak period in American judicial history. In light of this decision, the government announced on December 18, 1944, the end of internment of all loyal Japanese Americans.

The Corrosive Nature of Camp

Unlike Hirabayashi, Yasui, Korematsu, and Endo, thousands of Japanese American internees lacked the inclination or opportunity to legally protest their imprisonment. But, as time went on, they began to express their fear, uncertainty, and disillusionment in dozens of ways. Gambling and prostitution, facts of life in any community, became seri-

During the war, internment resisters (from left to right) Fred Korematsu, Minoru Yasui, and Gordon Hirabayashi, shown here during a press conference in 1983, challenged the legality of the government's actions against Japanese Americans.

ous problems. Petty theft became more common. As Yoshiko Uchida writes:

> [T]he corrosive nature of life in camp seemed to bring out the worst in many people, provoking them into doing things they probably would not have done outside. There was shoplifting in the dry goods store and false receipts were turned in for rebate at the Canteen. . . . One of our neighbors narrowly escaped being attacked as she crossed the high school lot one night, and women no longer felt safe walking alone after dark.[106]

Stress on Families

With the passing months, other negative reactions became noticeable. Tempers regularly gave way. Manners deteriorated. Tension grew between family members who were forced to live in close quarters. Charles Kikuchi observed, "We tried to thrash this whole matter of the increasing number of petty arguments out and find the reasons for them. [My sister] Alice just can't or won't realize that they are due to the unsettled minds of the people who fear for the future. That is why Mom nags so much one day and then is so kind the next."[107]

The communal aspects of the camps also undermined family relationships and created stress. At meals, men would sit with men, women with women. Young people abandoned their parents and joined friends, sitting at different tables and sometimes eating at different halls. Jeanne Wakatsuki Houston recalls the breakdown of manners and her brother's rowdy behavior. "Younger boys, like Ray, would make a game of seeing how many mess halls they could hit in one meal period—be the first in line at Block 16, gobble down your food, run to 17 by the middle of the dinner hour . . . and hurry to 18 to make the end of that chow line."[108]

Internees line up for dinner in the Heart Mountain mess hall. Children often left their parents during mealtime to eat with friends; slowly, the communal nature of the camps weakened family bonds.

Nisei Versus Issei

The stress of internment affected most personal relationships to some degree, but it produced serious tension between the older and younger generations. Part of this was due to the fact that many Issei had married later in life; thus the age gap was unusually wide between parents and children. In addition, the Issei, once breadwinners in the family, no longer needed to provide for their families. Charles Kikuchi observed, "The role of the Issei father in the family life has become less dominant because he no longer holds the economic purse strings. . . . Before, this has

been the source of their power and it carried a lot of weight."[109]

In addition, many Nisei males in their twenties and thirties now assumed positions of leadership primarily because they spoke English and thus were better able to fill out forms and relay important information. Entrusted with such responsibilities, most lost the respectful attitudes they had once shown their elders and boldly stated their opinions when discussions about personal behavior, family interaction, or camp policy arose.

Hurt and humiliated by their loss of power, the Issei often retaliated by withdrawing from family life and by taunting their children that their citizenship had not kept them out of the camps. The Nisei, on the other hand, condemned the closemindedness of the older generation who criticized American policies. Charles Kikuchi confessed, "It gripes me no end to think of being confined in the same place with these Japanists. If they could only realize that in spite of all their past mistreatments, they have not done so bad in America because of the democratic traditions—with its faults." [110]

Social Disputes

Tension and strife within families and between generations was not the only reaction to betrayal that surfaced in the camps. Over time, problems arose that ranged from minor disputes to near riots. In Heart Mountain center in Wyoming, internee anger over low wages resulted in several strikes, which were broken only after the strike leaders were sent to an Arizona internment camp. In Topaz Relocation Center, a group of pro-Japanese Issei and Kibei began making threats against community council leaders who they believed were cooperating too closely with the camp administration. Yoshiko Uchida writes, "The harassment of Issei leaders increased, and one of the church ministers who also devoted much time to community service was attacked one night by three masked men wielding lead pipes." [111]

Death at Manzanar

Anger and disillusionment festered in many camps, but Manzanar was the site of some of the most violent outbreaks. There, a large militant faction, led by embittered war veteran

The Nisei Future

Tension between older and younger generations often stemmed from the fact that the Nisei saw themselves as present and future leaders of the Japanese American community. Charles Kikuchi describes this point of view in The Kikuchi Diary.

"Babe [a friend] and I thought that the Issei must recognize the fact that this was principally the Nisei future and that they should not try to dominate the picture. . . . Babe is opposed to having the Issei in the picture. 'It's about time they realized that we can't always be bowing to their wishes. Some of us are getting to be 35 and 40 years old and why should we not try to develop the responsibility? The Issei group are too old and it will be the Nisei who are going to support them after the war. I was in business with an Issei and just because he was older he wanted to run everything his own way. He didn't want to keep books, but I made him. It was a good thing because when December 7 came around everything was in order. Otherwise he would have had a lot of embarrassing questions to answer and he would have been sunk. It's the same thing here. Sure, they are older, but they don't know any more about this new problem than we do. We are the ones to do the work and they must recognize the fact that we have to take a firm stand in this whole business.'"

Joe Kurihara, loudly opposed some Japanese American camp leaders' policies. As months passed, food shortages and rumors that sugar was being stolen by Caucasian cooks and sold on the black market added to the internees' unhappiness and brought tension to the breaking point.

Finally, on December 5, 1942 (almost one year after Pearl Harbor), several militants attacked and beat a prominent JACL leader who they believed was an informant. The assailants were taken into custody and jailed outside the center. The next day, Kurihara called a mass meeting of internees, during which speakers urged a full-scale takeover of the camp and threatened bloodshed if the assailants were not released.

In an effort to maintain control, center director Ralph Merritt declared martial law. When the mob grew belligerent, military police took action. One former internee remembers, "The MP fired shots into the defenseless crowd. A classmate, Jimmy Ito, was shot and killed. It was a terrifying experience."[112]

During the incident, another internee was killed, and several others were wounded. The mob eventually dispersed, but tension ran high for several weeks. Calm returned only after leaders of the riot were arrested and transferred to a high security camp.

A Question of Loyalty

Tension in the centers reached new heights in January 1943, after the government distributed a form entitled "Application for Leave Clearance" to all internees over the age of seventeen. The procedure, intended to identify those qualified for military service and to speed up resettlement out of the camps, only added to many internees' confusion and resentment. Page Smith writes in

Democracy on Trial, "If the War Relocation Authority had had the most malevolent of intentions it could not have found a better way to sow dissension and worse among the inhabitants of the centers."[113]

The four-page document required everyone to answer a series of questions. Trouble arose over Question 27 and Question 28. The first, directed at draft-age males, asked: "Are you willing to serve in the armed forces of the United States on combat duty, wherever ordered?" Women were asked if they would be willing to join the WACs or the Army Nurse Corps. Question 28, to be answered by all internees, asked, "Will you swear unqualified allegiance to the United States of America and faithfully defend the United States from any or all attack by foreign or domestic forces, and forswear any form of allegiance or obedience to the Japanese emperor, or any other foreign government, power, or organization?"

Division and Disorder

No one had foreseen the division and disorder the registration forms would produce. Center residents were already hostile toward the government that had assumed from the first that they were untrustworthy and treacherous. They resented that it now demanded their loyalty and asked them to fight for the principles of freedom and justice which they had been denied. One draft-age Nisei asked, "Why should I [fight for my country] when the government has taken away our rights and locked us up like a bunch of criminals?"[114] Some men hesitated to vote "yes" for fear they were volunteering for military service and would have to leave their families to an uncertain fate in the camps. Others noted the title of the registration form and feared that a "yes" vote would force them to leave

The Democratic Process

The government's loyalty questionnaire caused serious controversy in the camps, turning father against son and brother against brother. The episode was a lesson in democracy, however, for people like Tom Kawaguchi, who explains his newfound insight in John Tateishi's And Justice for All.

"I was a loyal American and I wanted to prove that the Japanese Americans were real Americans, just like anybody else. And this is what a lot of my friends didn't understand. When this yes-yes, no-no business took place, I was disappointed in some of them who went no-no. It took me a number of years, but I suddenly realized that a no-no answer was all part of the democratic process, that somebody else had his choice and I had my choice. We had some problems in camp because some people wanted to go as a block and say no-no. We had a considerable amount of discussion on that, because we have our own individual rights and we can express ourselves any way we want to."

the centers while other family members who voted "no" would be forced to stay.

To complicate matters, questions in the document were phrased in such a way that several interpretations were possible. Nisei pointed out that they, as U.S. citizens, had never sworn allegiance to Japan and therefore did not have to forswear (or renounce) that loyalty. By doing so, they might appear to have once harbored disloyal thoughts about America. The Issei, on the other hand, had not been allowed to become citizens. Most were loyal to America, but they feared that, if they renounced their homeland, they would essentially be people without a country. Registration officials quickly realized the unfairness of this question and changed it to read, "Will you swear to abide by the laws of the United States and to take no action which would . . . interfere with the war effort?" Most were happy to agree to such a statement.

Yes-Yes, No-No

Since internees could only speculate over the government's true motive for registration, they argued at length over the best answers to give. Some of the most cautious took the questions at face value and claimed the best answer would be "yes" to both, even if that meant going into the army and leaving vulnerable family members behind. They feared that those who answered "no" would lose their citizenship and be deported to Japan. The more daring looked at the questionnaire as an opportunity to vent their anger to the government. This group declared they would vote "yes-yes" only if they were first treated like real citizens and released from camp. For those who saw both sides, the decision was an agonizing one, as one former internee remembers:

> Here I was, a 19-year-old, having to make a decision that would affect the welfare of the whole family. If I signed "no, no," I would throw away my citizenship and force my sisters and brother to do the same. Being the oldest son . . . it was up to me to take care of my parents, sisters, and brothers. It was about a mile to the administration building. I can still remember vividly. Every step I took, I questioned

Japanese Education

Classified as a member of a "disloyal" family, thirteen-year-old internee Ben Takeshita recalls his life at Tule Lake Relocation Center after he and his family were transferred from Topaz in September 1943. Even those youth who were not a part of the militant movement at Tule Lake were forced to take part in pro-Japanese activities as a daily routine.

"So they exposed us to Japanese culture and Japanese education, as they understood it. Kibeis [Japanese Americans educated in Japan] taught us and used methods like making you sit on the floor for an hour, and if you moved you got hit on the head. This kind of thing. They were definitely serious. . . . We had no choice, we knew who the boss was and we just went along and went to Japanese school. All day we were in Japanese school. We were learning the language and being hit. The school forbade speaking any English; you had to speak only Japanese even at home. So when we came home and our friends . . . came over and we started talking English with them, the teachers next door would hear and the next day come around and say, 'You spoke English.' So we would be made examples of, and we would definitely be hit harder—with the ends of those cot beds. We soon learned to speak Japanese."

myself, shall I sign it "no, no," or "no, yes." The walk seemed like it took hours.[115]

Registration eventually took on such importance that internees identified each other by the way they had voted. Friends disagreed and turned against one another. Fathers and sons stopped speaking. As one former internee recalls, "The resulting infighting, beatings, and verbal abuses left families torn apart, parents against children, brothers against sisters. . . . So bitter was all this that even to this day, there are many amongst us who do not speak about that period."[116]

Segregation

The internees' concerns were somewhat justified by the government's reaction to their answers. Those who answered "no-no" were classed as disloyal and segregated, moved into a camp where they could be more closely guarded and where they would not influence loyal internees. Tule Lake center in northern California was chosen since it contained the largest number of disloyals when the votes were tabulated.

By the end of October 1943, Tule Lake was classed as a "segregation center" and had been converted into a maximum security facility with tall barbed wire fences, quarters to hold one thousand soldiers, and six tanks parked around the perimeter. To make space for "disloyals," officials transferred six thousand "loyal" Tule Lake residents to other camps, although some refused to go, either because they did not want to leave California or because they were tired of moving.

Some of the newcomers were pro-Japanese militants who were judged real threats to the security of the United States. Included in this category were some of the Kibei, who had been educated in Japan. Others, however, were peace-loving men and women who, out of fear, disillusionment, or confusion, had voted "no" on the registration form. A third category were those people—many of them women and children—who had followed their "disloyal" family member out of other camps.

Tule Lake

Arriving at Tule Lake, internees encountered conditions as grim and depressing as was the rock-and-sagebrush setting of the center. Rainfall in northern California was scant, but snow fell in the winter, and temperatures often dropped below freezing. The camp was well fortified against escape, but it was poorly equipped to shelter the numbers of residents confined within its barbed wire borders. Barracks were overcrowded. Bathrooms were long distances from living quarters. Health care was minimal, and food was poor and in short supply. One government official wrote:

> The barbed-wire [fence] surrounding the 18,000 people there was like that of the prison camps of the Germans. There were the same turrets for the soldiers and the same machine guns for those who might attempt to climb the high wiring. . . .

> The buildings were covered with tarred paper over green and shrinking shiplap—this for the low winter temperatures of the high elevation of Tule Lake. . . . No federal penitentiary so treats its adult prisoners. Here were the children and babies as well.[117]

Growing Resentment

As time passed, Tule Lake residents grew increasingly resentful of these harsh condi-

tions. Some blamed food shortages on the Caucasian staff, which was allegedly smuggling food out of camp and selling it on the black market. Some were angry at center director Raymond Best, who showed himself particularly insensitive to their requests that conditions be improved. By late 1943, there had been protests, strikes, and demonstrations led by militants who could sometimes draw a crowd of ten thousand.

With feelings running so high, Best declared martial law and called in the army. Then, for three months, tanks rolled through the grounds, military police lobbed tear gas at innocent internees standing in line for water or coal, and camp authorities performed unannounced midnight inspections of barracks for knives, scissors, and other potential weapons. Innocent residents grew increasingly hostile, and pro-Japanese feelings grew stronger. When at one meeting, one man tried to communicate in English, the crowd cheered the leader's reply: "This is Japan. Who dares to speak English here?"[118]

The Stockade

Residents who were unlucky enough to be arrested by the military police at Tule Lake usually ended up in the stockade, a prison for troublemakers within the camp. Sanitary conditions there were primitive, visitors were excluded, and detainees were sometimes beaten and brutalized. Men in the "bull pen"—a higher security area within the stockade itself—suffered from infected wounds and slept on the ground in tents with no heat. Tokio Yamane, a former inmate, recalls, "For the first time in our lives, those of us confined to the 'bull pen' experienced a life and death struggle for survival."[119]

Since communication between the stockade and the camp was forbidden, worried family members often went months at a time not knowing if their loved ones were dead or alive. Help finally arrived in July 1944 when Ernest Besig, the director of the ACLU in northern California, investigated conditions at the center, determined that serious abuse was taking place, and promptly hired San Francisco attorney Wayne Collins to secure the release of the stockade prisoners. After Collins threatened to go public with the story, center officials gave in to his demands. When Collins visited Tule Lake in August 1944, he was satisfied to find that the stockade had been demolished. He observed, "There was no vestige of the Stockade then discernible. Even the fence that surrounded it was gone." [120]

"Pressure Boys"

Despite the repressive methods used to control troublemakers at Tule Lake, Raymond Best allowed several militant, pro-Japanese associations to become influential in center activities. He rationalized that since many "disloyals" would probably choose to go to Japan after the war, they should be allowed to pursue a Japanese lifestyle in the center if they so desired.

The militants' outlook was similar to Best's. They believed that the future for all Japanese Americans lay in Japan, and, with that in mind, they set out to convince as many residents as possible to prepare for such a move. Japanese language schools were established and all young people were forced to attend. Young men were encouraged to shave their heads in traditional Japanese military style and join militant organizations. Internees were strongly "encouraged" to enroll in classes that taught Japanese manners and cooking, flower arrangement, painting, and calligraphy. Michi Weglyn notes that others worked to learn the discipline of a "true Japanese." "Under the direction of Kibei drillmasters, open-air calisthenics and cold showers became a regular 6 A.M. ritual in many of the blocks." [121]

There was some resistance to such coercion, especially from young Nisei who were the most Americanized and who had no desire to leave the United States. Outspoken criticism was countered by violence from the militants, however, so most resisted passively by speaking English to one another and by locking themselves in their rooms during demonstrations. The "pressure boys," as they were

Attorney Wayne Collins helped to bring order to the raucous Tule Lake center. Collins continued to help Japanese Americans during and after the war.

Members of the pro-Japanese association Hokoku Seinen Dan gather at the gate to Tule Lake to give a "banzai" send-off to members who are being sent to the Justice Department camp in Santa Fe, New Mexico.

called, seemed to be everywhere, however. One desperate internee wrote, "The fanatical groups seemed to know everyone's act and nothing seemed confidential in this congested center."[122] Another remembers, "It wasn't long before everyone who had no intention at first, were coerced to become a member. . . . We had no other choice for we had no way of moving out or away from terrorism in this fenced-in concentration camp."[123]

Renunciation

Not only were residents urged to think and act Japanese, but militants insisted that true followers would even go so far as to renounce their U.S. citizenship in their efforts to get to Japan. Ironically, their views were given weight by the actions of government officials who succeeded in passing a denaturalization bill in July 1944. Written specifically with Japanese Americans in mind, the bill allowed citizens living on American soil to renounce their citizenship in times of war. The policy had not been on the books previously, since lawmakers feared that war hysteria could lead citizens to make hasty, poorly thought out decisions.

Such was the case at Tule Lake. To harassed and discouraged internees, the denaturalization bill seemed the best answer to their problems, especially since many were again frightened by rumors that those who did not renounce their citizenship would be thrown out of the center into the midst of hostile Caucasians. The government announcement of camp closures, which came in the middle of the crisis, did nothing to soothe such fears.

Pressured by pro-Japanese groups, driven by fear, and gambling that they would be allowed to stay at least temporarily with family and friends if they renounced their citizenship, internees at Tule Lake began a mass renunciation movement in mid-1944. One former internee remembers, "One (thing) that put a scare into me was that families would be separated. To me, I just had to sign on that paper. . . . I have regretted that I took such a drastic step . . . but I was afraid if I was torn away from the family I would never see them again in this uncertain world."[124]

The Consequences of a Terrible Mistake

Almost 6,000 Tule Lake residents renounced their U.S. citizenship and asked to return to Japan; the combined total from all other camps was only 128. Center administration tried halfheartedly to persuade renunciants (those who renounced) to rethink their decisions, but few did so at the time.

By March 1945, however, the number of renunciations grew so large that the WRA took action. Officials at Tule Lake were directed to round up radical pro-Japanese leaders and send them to Justice Department camps. With their departure, the tone of the center changed. Intimidation and pro-Japanese activities came to an end. Fear and frenzy died down. The internees had time to think about what they had done.

The consequences were horrifying. Most now realized that they had made a terrible mistake signing away their citizenship and their right to remain in America. The United States, for all its shortcomings, was still their homeland. They wanted nothing more than to remain.

All they could do to correct the situation, however, was to beg the government to cancel their requests. One man pleaded with the Justice Department, "[M]y wife's citizenship is gone. . . . She did not renounce out of disloyalty. She would never do anything against this country. . . . Don't you see how awful our situation is? Do help us if you can."[125]

But reversing what they had done was not easy. As officials prepared to close the centers, as other internees stood on the brink of freedom, the government classified the renunciants as enemy aliens and instituted a removal process that would take them back to Japan. For many, it would be years before the mistake they made could be remedied.

By the autumn of 1944, the presumed need for mass exclusion of Japanese Americans from the West Coast was past. Disloyals had been identified and segregated into Tule Lake Center. Allied forces had crippled Japan's air force and defeated its navy in the Battle of Leyte Gulf in late October. A Japanese invasion of the West Coast was no longer even a remote possibility.

At the same time, protest was mounting in the United States over the unconstitutional treatment of Japanese American citizens. Public opinion turned against General DeWitt, who was dubbed a "military zealot" by the *Washington Post*; in late 1943 he was relieved of his Western Defense Command. That same year Attorney General Francis Biddle, who had opposed relocation from the beginning, wrote, "[T]he present practice of keeping loyal American citizens in concentration camps for longer than is necessary is dangerous and repugnant to the principles of our Government."[126] Secretary of the Interior Harold Ickes wrote to the president on June 1, 1944, "The continued exclusion of American citizens of Japanese ancestry from the affected areas is clearly unconstitutional in the present circumstances."[127]

A New Beginning for Japanese Americans

Finally, as the Supreme Court ruled in favor of Mitsuye Endo in December 1944, the exclusionary ban was lifted. Internment was over. All loyal Japanese Americans were now at liberty to return to their homes on the West Coast.

The decision to close the centers was not entirely unopposed, however. Anti-Japanese groups such as No Japs Incorporated in San Diego and the Pacific Coast Japanese Problem League in Los Angeles were ready to continue their fight to exclude Japanese Americans. An article in the *San Francisco Chronicle* urged President Roosevelt and the WRA to continue exclusion at least until the end of the war. "We believe . . . that to allow the Japanese to return during the war is inadvisable because it would cause riots, turmoil, bloodshed, and endanger the war effort,"[128] one editor wrote.

Ironically, many Japanese Americans shared those feelings. As one man said, "I don't want to be the first one to go back and get killed."[129] In addition to their fears of violence and discrimination, many internees admitted that they were too old and too tired to start over. They had no homes to return to and their families had been scattered. Most had formed close ties inside the camps. They were familiar with routines there, and more or less content with their lives. One resident observed, "We are told and encouraged to relocate again into the world as a stranger in strange communities! We now have lost all security. . . . Where shall we go? What shall we do at the twilight of the evening of our lives?"[130]

The Scouts

As time passed, however, camp residents became resigned to leaving. The WRA encouraged some of the bravest to go first, to visit their old neighborhoods and communities, and to report back on their findings. Historian Edward Spicer writes:

> The scouts went out for a week or two, looked over their old towns, interviewed many people, canvassed the possibilities for renewing their old lines of activity. They came back to the centers to add to the store of information that evacuees had been accumulating through correspondence with friends on the West Coast and through reading the hometown newspapers.[131]

Reports from the scouts were mixed. Some had been uncomfortable living among whites again and had been quick to notice signs of hostility. Homes were lost, stored possessions stolen or destroyed. Paul Shinoda, a Nisei from southern California, remembers, "We couldn't pack up all the stoves and refrigerators and stuff like that. We stored them away in the nursery [of our house]— our stove, our kids' toys, and some of our furniture. . . . When we got back from camp we had nothing—even the toys were all gone."[132] On the other hand, many scouts discovered that Caucasian neighbors and friends had been faithful trustees of their possessions. Some reported that they had even successfully reclaimed their land or their automobiles.

This was encouraging news. Soon, in every camp, increasing numbers of internees were making plans to return and resettle on the West Coast. One Issei wrote, "We're leaving the ninth (of October). We don't have a home to go back to and will have to stay at the hostel or at a hotel until we can find something else. I want to go back to Tacoma where I lived for a long time."[133]

Closing the Centers

With a twenty-five-dollar allowance from the government in their pockets, the internees left the camps throughout 1945; by the end of September, they were leaving at a rate of two thousand a week. Some returned home by bus. Many went by train. Jeanne Wakatsuki Houston's father purchased a cheap car for their move. She describes their departure in *Farewell to Manzanar*:

> A few days before we left Manzanar Papa decided that since we *had* to go, we might as well leave in style, and by our own volition. . . . Late that afternoon he came . . . in a midnight blue Nash sedan. . . . To get all nine of us, plus our clothes and the odds and ends of furniture we'd accumulated, from Owens Valley 225 miles south to Long Beach, Papa had to make the trip three times. He pushed the car so hard it broke down about every hundred miles or so. In all it took four days.[134]

The exodus left large gaps in remaining camp populations. As the once crowded blocks grew empty, the WRA began discontinuing those services it deemed unnecessary. Schools and businesses closed. Clubs disbanded. Newspapers went out of print. Mess halls were consolidated to the indignation of residents who had gotten used to the services of a particular cook and resisted seeing new faces at their dining tables. Edward Spicer writes, "People began to feel that the sub-

Former internees bid their friends farewell upon their release from a relocation center. Internment officially ended in December 1944, after the Supreme Court ruled internment of loyal citizens unconstitutional.

stance of block life was disintegrating.... There was a feeling of decay and decline in the air that weighed more and more on people through the summer.... As the blocks crumbled, the relocation centers began to disintegrate before people's eyes and under their feet."[135]

Faced with this disintegration, most internees found it less painful to leave the centers than to stay, although the Takagi family at Minidoka in Idaho had to be literally forced into a car, driven to the train station, and pushed onto the last train. All camps but Tule Lake, which was kept open to permit

Justice Department hearings, were finally closed by December 1945.

The Fight for Rights

Instead of resettling out of the camps in 1945 as other internees did, thousands of Tule Lake residents faced the consequences of renunciation. They were no longer U.S. citizens, and while the United States was still at war with Japan the government could legally keep them in captivity. In fact, at their own requests, most were slated to be sent to Japan

Resettlement was top priority with most internees, but many older Japanese Americans were comfortable with life in the camps and had to be physically removed, as this incident from Page Smith's Democracy on Trial *illustrates.*

"At Granada [Colorado], some of the older Issei refused to leave and were actually carried to the trains. A classic case of an evacuee refusing to leave was that of a man named Hirose. James Sakoda asked him his reasons. 'My record is clear,' he told Sakoda, 'and they (the center administrators) should know where I stand. When I was once questioned before, I told them I would not go any place unless the war was over and settled. . . . You say that the war has ended, but I don't think so. If it has ended there should be some news of the settlement reached between Japan and America. Until that occurs I can't leave the project. I've made that clear to the people at the office. . . .' When the center's internal police came to take Hirose to the railroad station, they found him hiding under his barracks. They thereupon locked his apartment and took him to the train, assuring him that they would pack his belongings and send them after him."

along with other "enemy aliens" who had been held in Justice Department camps during the course of the war.

The Justice Hearings

For those who regretted their actions, the arrival of San Francisco attorney Wayne Collins in July was a stroke of good fortune. Collins, a strong believer in civil rights, had come to the internees' aid in August 1944 over trouble in the stockade. A feisty Irishman, the attorney now threw himself into the fight to reinstate his clients' citizenship and to save them from deportation (removal from the United States).

In November 1945, Collins filed two mass petitions in U.S. district court in San Francisco, claiming that his clients had been unduly influenced by terrorist pressures while in government custody at Tule Lake. Because the government had done nothing to protect them from that intimidation, he argued, decisions to give up their citizenship were invalid.

Several months later, in July 1946, officials from the Justice Department arrived at Tule Lake to begin investigative hearings on the question of deportation. During the several months the hearings took place, over four thousand residents of Tule Lake voluntarily left for Japan. Others were eventually judged to be no danger to the United States and were allowed to resettle.

The Justice hearings did nothing to restore the citizenship to Collins's clients, however, so the attorney continued his fight in the courts. After many obstacles and setbacks, his battle ended successfully in 1968, twenty-three years after the suits were filed. Collins triumphantly wrote, "The fundamental rights, liberties, privileges and immunities of these citizens are now honored. The discrimination practiced against them by the government has ceased. The episode which constituted an infamous chapter in our history has come to a close." [136]

A New Life

Japanese Americans who returned to the West Coast after internment could not help but notice the many changes that had occurred there during the war. Hundreds of thousands of people had moved to California from other parts of the country. Farms which had once been leased by Japanese Americans were now run by refugees from the dust bowl. Sections of Los Angeles that had once been Japanese were now predominantly Black. Housing was expensive. The WRA provided little financial assistance to those leaving the camps, so many residents were forced to take shelter in trailer parks and low-rent apartment complexes, places they would have scorned before internment. In many cases, when one family found housing, they shared their quarters with homeless relatives and friends.

Jobs too were now hard to find, so returnees had no choice but to take what work they could get in order to survive. Young women often hired themselves out as maids and housekeepers, since those jobs usually included room and board. Former farm owners settled for being hired hands. Men such as Iwato Itow, who had been in training to become a master aviation

Repatriates embark for Japan on November 24, 1945. During the following year, four thousand internees from Tule Lake were voluntarily deported.

mechanic before the war, took jobs as manual laborers to support their families. Itow says, "I am bitter. There's a constant reminder of what I missed or lost out on because of the war. . . . My occupation now is gardener, and working the soil is one thing I wanted to get away from."[137]

As the scouts had discovered, hostility from white neighbors—threats, vandalism, thefts—was an ever-present menace in some areas. Shig Doi, who fought in the 442nd Regimental Combat Team in the war, had to ward off fire and shotgun attacks when he and his family returned to California to claim land they owned. The Fujimoro ranch house and barn in central California were burned in a suspicious nighttime fire.

Community Aid

For many Japanese Americans, their return to the West Coast was a more positive experience. In a few cases, the government itself provided emergency shelter in trailers and government housing for those who had nowhere to stay. Church groups once again aided those in need. In some towns, church meeting halls were turned into temporary hostels. More permanent hotels were set up by groups such as the Buddhist Brotherhood in America, the American Baptist Home Missionary Society, and the Japanese Methodist Church. As one member of the Federated Mission of Pasadena observed, "A young man coming here could stay at the church, get a job through the church's placement service and study English at their night school. There were quite a few people who received service and care from the church."[138]

As Japanese Americans began quietly slipping back into mainstream society, negative feelings in the white community gradually became more positive. The war had formally ended on September 2, 1945; Japan lay broken and defeated after the bombing of Hiroshima and Nagasaki. Nisei had served in the war and had proven their loyalty beyond question. The returnees seemed only to want to get on with their lives and live in peace.

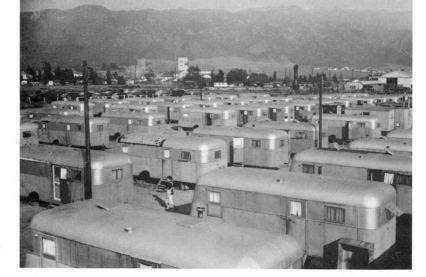

After leaving the camps, many Japanese Americans had no homes to which to return. This housing project in Burbank, California, provided trailers for returnees to live in until they found permanent housing.

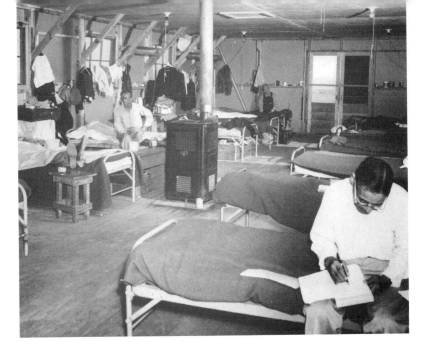

The interior of the men's dormitory at the Santa Ana Housing Project in California, where returning Japanese Americans were given temporary housing.

In fact, many Americans now felt guilty over their unfair treatment of Japanese Americans during the war. Community leaders, some of whom had once supported relocation, urged racial tolerance and tried to ensure that returnees receive fair treatment.

Ayaku Uyeda remembers when she and her family came back to Seattle:

Many of these people were worried that [we] might be hurt by other Americans. They said to let them know immediately

"Americans After All"

Disillusioned with America after their internment experience, a small number of Japanese Americans chose to renounce their citizenship and go to Japan in the belief that life there would be better. In many cases, that decision proved a sad mistake, as Page Smith relates in Democracy on Trial.

"The experiences of the renunciants and those repatriated to Japan make a strange and compelling story. They sailed back to a Japan that existed only in their dreams, a nation devastated by war, a nation in which, to their perplexity and confusion, they felt themselves aliens; they had to return to dis-cover that against any conscious intention, against their will, they had become Americans. . . . They had gone to Japan with the avowed intention of becoming wholly Japanese. Once there, they discovered that they were Americans after all. . . .

Violet de Cristoforo was one of those who was repatriated with her husband and found the experience profoundly disillusioning. 'The war devastated Japan, and we were not accepted in Japan either, first of all because we were different.' They were glad to return to the United States. Much the same story was repeated thousands of times."

Changing Attitudes

Former internee Wilson Makabe lost a leg while fighting with the 442nd Regimental Combat Team in Italy in 1943. He returned to the United States at the end of 1944 and later joined his father and sister in their northern California home. In John Tateishi's And Justice for All, *Makabe relates an episode that illustrates changing Caucasian attitudes after the war.*

"One of the fellows had a service station, and when I first came back, I went into this station. I knew the family. The fellow's father was one of the old settlers in Loomis and knew my father well. When he saw me at the service station getting out, struggling to get out of the car, to fill it with gas, he came out. After I was all through he said, 'I'd like to talk to you.' I said, 'Hop in.' He traveled with me down the road from the station. He said, 'Y'know I was one [lousy person]. I had signs on my service station saying "No Jap trade wanted."' He said, 'Now, when I see you come back like that, I feel so small.' And he was crying. That was one of my experiences when I came back."

if there was any trouble. They said that the war was not a crime that we committed so don't be ashamed or scared of anybody. Because of this type of support, we were able to resettle fairly smoothly.[139]

The returnees themselves did all they could to convince others of their peaceful intentions. Many resettled in cities, where community services were better and where they were less noticeable and more easily accepted. All worked hard to reestablish businesses and to rebuild their lives.

Patience, tolerance, and a willingness to put aside past wrongs were important factors that contributed to the smooth reentry of Japanese Americans into society. As a result, however, internment soon was all but forgotten by many Americans. The episode was not mentioned in history books. Officials who had supported it now saw it as a mistake best ignored. The internees who remembered their imprisonment as a time of unbearable humiliation did not speak of it, even to their children. As John Tateishi writes, "They could not find the voice within themselves to tell others, often even their children, about what had happened to them personally. And so the victims exiled themselves to a silence that lasted forty years."[140]

Liberty and Justice for All

As decades passed, many Japanese Americans discovered that they could not forget their years in the camps. The experience had changed their assumptions, their attitudes, and their expectations. Silence was not helping to heal the emotional and mental scars that many carried.

New generations of Japanese Americans had also begun to ask questions about internment. They had heard their parents and grandparents talk about life before and after the camps, but of the central event itself they knew very little. Those who had gleaned a few facts wondered how their parents and grandparents had allowed themselves to be deprived of freedom without a fight. Why had they—American citizens—docilely given up their rights when the government was so obviously in the wrong?

Making a Claim

Faced with such questions, the quiet Americans finally decided to speak out. They began talking to their children and writing about their experiences. Some even returned to the deserted ruins of the camp sites in memory of the years of hardship. As they did, they began to accept the fact that they had not been to blame for what they had suffered. Their shame and bitterness lessened. Many even came to the conclusion that the government had an obligation to make amends for what it had done.

The government, aware that internment had not only been unfair but unconstitutional, had already taken limited steps to grant Japanese Americans certain rights and privileges they had been denied before and during the war. The Walter-McCarran Immigration and Naturalization Act of 1952 had lifted the ban on immigration from Asian countries and allowed Japanese and other Asians to enter the United States every year. The act also allowed people of Japanese ancestry to become naturalized U.S. citizens, and revoked other discriminatory laws that had been on the books for years.

Under the Evacuation Claims Act of 1948, Japanese Americans could file claims for tangible losses experienced during internment. Monetary restitution had been severely limited under this act, however. Although total loss of material possessions in the Japanese American community was estimated to be $400 million, less than $40 million was reimbursed by the government. By 1965, when the last claim was paid, each claimant had received about one-tenth of what they had lost. There had been no allowance made for mental suffering, physical hardships, or death of loved ones.

As former internees who had been children in the camps reached adulthood, they grew less satisfied with such minimal reparation. More outspoken than their parents, they claimed that the government had shirked its responsibilities, both in terms of apologies and monetary compensation. They believed

Japanese men and women are sworn in as U.S. citizens in San Francisco in 1953. The Walter-McCarran Immigration and Naturalization Act of 1952 allowed people of Japanese lineage to become naturalized citizens.

that, just as the government had repaid American hostages for their ordeal in Iran and Native Americans for generations of broken treaties, so it should make fair and reasonable amends to Japanese Americans. A small but determined group of individuals, led by the JACL, decided to approach the government on behalf of all those who had lost so much during internment.

"Liberty Is Priceless"

Efforts by the JACL to persuade the government to investigate their claims were successful in July 1980, at which time Congress authorized the formation of the Commission on Wartime Relocation and Internment of Civilians. For several months in 1981, the

commission (a nine-member multiethnic body made up of former members of Congress, senators, Supreme Court justices, and respected civic leaders) reviewed internment-related documents and memoranda and interviewed more than seven hundred persons, including former internees. Its findings, published in the report *Personal Justice Denied*, were conclusive. The creation of Executive Order 9066 had not been justified by military necessity. There had never been a need for relocation. The report stated, "A grave injustice was done to American citizens and resident aliens of Japanese ancestry who . . . were excluded, removed and detained by the United States during World War II."[141] The commission recommended that restitution in the amount of $20,000 be made to each of the survivors of internment.

Many Japanese Americans were offended by the recommendation, viewing it as a form of welfare. Some believed that the government assumed that every Japanese American had had equal losses during the war. Others felt that no amount of money could make up for past suffering. Most, however, shared the view of Norman Mineta, who spent his early life in the camps:

I realize that there are some who say that these payments are inappropriate. Liberty is priceless, they say, and you cannot put a price on freedom. That's an easy statement when you have your freedom. But to say that because constitutional rights are priceless they really have no value at all is to turn the argument on its head. Would I sell my civil and constitutional rights for $20,000? No. But having had those rights ripped away from me, do I think I am entitled to compensation? Absolutely.[142]

In October 1990, former internees received a letter from President George Bush, in which he apologized for injustices of the past and promised to uphold the rights of all individuals in the future. That same month, the first reparation checks began arriving in the mail. More than forty-eight years had passed since internment had ended. In the end, some form of justice was finally done.

Former internees will always look upon internment as a bleak period of history, but

Painful Memories

As years passed, many former internees made pilgrimages to the camps, to heal their emotional wounds and to pay tribute to so many who spent years behind barbed wire. Jeanne Wakatsuki Houston was eleven years old when she left Manzanar. In Farewell to Manzanar, *she relates her feelings on returning to the camp twenty-five years later.*

"Manzanar was the biggest city between Reno and Los Angeles, a special kind of western boom town that sprang from the sand, flourished, had its day, and now has all but disappeared. The barracks are gone, torn down right after the war. The guard towers are gone, and the mess halls and shower rooms, the hospital, the tea gardens, and the white buildings outside the compound. Even the dust is gone. Spreading brush holds it to the ground. Thirty years earlier, army bulldozers had scraped everything clean to start construction. . . .

We were crossing what used to be a firebreak, now a sandy field devoid of any growth. . . . The firebreak was where we had talent shows and dances and outdoor movies in the summer, and where the kids played games. . . . I closed my eyes and I was ten years old again. Nothing had changed. . . .

Until this trip I had not been able to admit that my own life really began there. The times I thought I had dreamed it were one way of getting rid of it, part of wanting to lose it, part of what you might call a whole Manzanar mentality I had lived with for twenty-five years. Much more than a remembered place, it had become a state of mind. Now, having seen it . . . having found it, I could say what you can only say when you've truly come to know a place: Farewell."

some now admit that something positive did come from the experience. Younger generations forced to break with age-old family traditions assimilated more easily into mainstream society. Those who moved east expanded their horizons, escaped from all-Japanese communities, and experienced life free of discrimination. All were challenged to examine their beliefs and loyalties and learned firsthand the strengths and weaknesses of democracy.

As a group, the majority of internees came through the experience with greater dignity and fewer emotional scars than experts might predict. Divorce rates, crime rates, and alcoholism did not rise alarmingly after internment. Rather, on leaving the camps, most people reestablished productive routines similar to those they had followed before internment. Many went on to contribute to society as loyal, hardworking citizens, some as responsible civic and community leaders.

Members of the younger generation who benefited from this successful reintegration give credit not only to increased tolerance from American society, but to the attitudes of older Japanese Americans who instilled values of diligence and cooperation in their children. Michi Weglyn writes:

> After all was said and done . . . it was the residual dignity of their elders which prevented disaster from becoming a catastrophe. . . . It was the hardy, enduring Issei who made possible the reversal of a crushing humiliation into an ultimate demonstration of triumph. How? . . . By continuing to stress patience, obedience, and duty more than rights. By demanding of one another the subordination of self to the larger interest. By urging in their children unstinting allegiance to their country . . . right or wrong.[143]

Renewing a Commitment

Monetary compensation and a formal apology from the government were long in coming, but beginning in October 1990 each surviving internee received a reparation check for $20,000.00. Accompanying each check was a copy of the following letter signed by President George Bush, published in Japanese Americans: From Relocation to Redress.

"The White House
Washington

A monetary sum and words alone cannot restore lost years or erase painful memories; neither can they fully convey our Nation's resolve to rectify injustice and to uphold the rights of individuals. We can never fully right the wrongs of the past. But we can take a clear stand for justice and recognize that serious injustices were done to Japanese Americans during World War II.

In enacting a law calling for restitution and offering a sincere apology, your fellow Americans have, in a very real sense, renewed their traditional commitment to the ideals of freedom, equality, and justice. You and your family have our best wishes for the future.

Sincerely,

George Bush"

The Yamamotos (pictured), former internees at Gila River Relocation Center, opened this lunch counter in Los Angeles after their release. Despite the hardships Japanese Americans endured during their internment, most reestablished their lives and businesses after the war.

Lessons to Be Learned

John Tateishi writes in his book *And Justice for All*, "The Japanese American internment was an experience unparalleled in the history of the United States."[144] Such an experience has little redeeming value, but former internees believe that it can provide valuable lessons for the future. First, it shows that Americans cannot always take the protection and security of their government for granted. Despite the checks and balances of the Constitution, injustices can be committed. Presidents, elected officials, and judges can be swayed by popular opinion.

Next, it teaches that Americans must be on guard against prejudice and discrimination. There will always be men such as General DeWitt and groups such as the Japanese Exclusion League that pose a threat to freedom and constitutional rights. If no one takes the time or makes the effort to speak out against such threats, innocent people will suffer.

Former residents of the camps are determined that Japanese Americans will never again be victims of such discrimination. They and their children continue to promote community pride, to remind others of their past, and to ensure that other minorities are not similarly betrayed. As Minoru Yasui wrote in the early 1980s:

Forty years later, we are still struggling to find means whereby this kind of thing can never happen again to any group of people. Tremendous outrages were inflicted upon us. We cannot rest, we shall not rest until we make every effort to assure that it shall never happen again.[145]

Notes

Introduction: The "Quiet Americans"

1. Quoted in Anne Reeploeg Fisher, *Exile of a Race*. Seattle: F. & T. Publishers, 1965, p. 35.
2. Quoted in Commission on Wartime Relocation and Internment of Civilians, *Personal Justice Denied*. Washington: GPO, 1982, p. 81.
3. Quoted in Thomas James, *Exile Within*. Cambridge, MA: Harvard University Press, 1987, pp. 23, 25.
4. Quoted in John Armor and Peter Wright, *Manzanar*. New York: Times Books, 1988, p. 58.
5. Quoted in Eric D. Johnson, "'Quiet Americans' Remember Pain," *Pierce County Herald*, October 1, 1985, p. 10.
6. Quoted in John Tateishi, ed., *And Justice for All*. New York: Random House, 1984, p. 15.

Chapter 1: Latecomers to America

7. Commission on Wartime Relocation, *Personal Justice Denied*, p. 45.
8. Roger Daniels, *Concentration Camps U.S.A.* New York: Holt, Rinehart & Winston, 1972, p. 5.
9. Quoted in Daniels, *Concentration Camps U.S.A.*, pp. 6–7.
10. Quoted in Page Smith, *Democracy on Trial*. New York: Simon & Schuster, 1995, p. 55.
11. Quoted in Armor and Wright, *Manzanar*, p. 5.
12. Quoted in Commission on Wartime Relocation, *Personal Justice Denied*, p. 32.
13. Quoted in Commission on Wartime Relocation, *Personal Justice Denied*, p. 34.

14. Yoshiko Uchida, *Desert Exile*. Seattle: University of Washington Press, 1982, p. 6.
15. Quoted in Smith, *Democracy on Trial*, p. 64.
16. Uchida, *Desert Exile*, pp. 36, 40.
17. Uchida, *Desert Exile*, pp. 41–42.
18. Quoted in Daniels, *Concentration Camps U.S.A.*, p. 23.
19. Quoted in Daniels, *Concentration Camps U.S.A.*, p. 24.
20. Daniels, *Concentration Camps U.S.A.*, p. 25.

Chapter 2: "What Is Going to Happen to Us?"

21. Quoted in Tateishi, *And Justice for All*, p. 168.
22. John Modell, ed., *The Kikuchi Diary*. Urbana: University of Illinois Press, 1973, pp. 42–43.
23. Quoted in Commission on Wartime Relocation, *Personal Justice Denied*, p. 52.
24. Quoted in Michi Weglyn, *Years of Infamy*. New York: William Morrow, Quill Paperbacks, 1976, p. 45.
25. Uchida, *Desert Exile*, pp. 46–47.
26. Quoted in Commission on Wartime Relocation, *Personal Justice Denied*, p. 69.
27. Quoted in Armor and Wright, *Manzanar*, p. 38.
28. Quoted in Roger Daniels, *Prisoners Without Trial*. New York: Hill & Wang, 1993, p. 38.
29. Quoted in Smith, *Democracy on Trial*, pp. 120–21.
30. Uchida, *Desert Exile*, p. 52.

31. Quoted in Armor and Wright, *Manzanar*, p. 20.
32. Quoted in Armor and Wright, *Manzanar*, p. 21.
33. Quoted in Armor and Wright, *Manzanar*, p. 22.
34. Quoted in Commission on Wartime Relocation, *Personal Justice Denied*, p. 82.
35. Quoted in Smith, *Democracy on Trial*, p. 127.
36. Jeanne Wakatsuki Houston and James D. Houston, *Farewell to Manzanar*. Boston: Houghton Mifflin, 1973, p. 13.
37. Quoted in Tateishi, *And Justice for All*, p. 147.
38. Quoted in Smith, *Democracy on Trial*, p. 146.
39. Quoted in Smith, *Democracy on Trial*, p. 146.
40. Quoted in Weglyn, *Years of Infamy*, p. 122.
41. Quoted in Weglyn, *Years of Infamy*, p. 122.
42. Quoted in Smith, *Democracy on Trial*, p. 151.
43. Quoted in Smith, *Democracy on Trial*, p. 151.
44. Quoted in Tateishi, *And Justice for All*, p. 169.
45. Quoted in Weglyn, *Years of Infamy*, p. 104.
46. Quoted in Weglyn, *Years of Infamy*, p. 103.
47. Quoted in Armor and Wright, *Manzanar*, p. 9.

Chapter 3: Protective Custody

48. Quoted in Commission on Wartime Relocation, *Personal Justice Denied*, p. 135.
49. Uchida, *Desert Exile*, p. 63.
50. Quoted in Tateishi, *And Justice for All*, p. 9.

51. Uchida, *Desert Exile*, pp. 61–62.
52. Quoted in Tateishi, *And Justice for All*, p. 215.
53. Uchida, *Desert Exile*, pp. 60–61.
54. Quoted in Tateishi, *And Justice for All*, p. 102.
55. Quoted in Weglyn, *Years of Infamy*, p. 78.
56. Uchida, *Desert Exile*, p. 70.
57. Quoted in Tateishi, *And Justice for All*, p. 73.
58. Quoted in Tateishi, *And Justice for All*, pp. 73–74.
59. Quoted in Tateishi, *And Justice for All*, pp. 12–13.
60. Uchida, *Desert Exile*, pp. 72, 75.
61. Modell, *The Kikuchi Diary*, p. 222.
62. Houston, *Farewell to Manzanar*, p. 25.
63. Quoted in Smith, *Democracy on Trial*, p. 245.
64. Houston, *Farewell to Manzanar*, p. 35.
65. Modell, *The Kikuchi Diary*, p. 82.
66. Quoted in Smith, *Democracy on Trial*, p. 249.
67. Modell, *The Kikuchi Diary*, p. 107.
68. Quoted in Commission on Wartime Relocation, *Personal Justice Denied*, p. 175.
69. Quoted in Weglyn, *Years of Infamy*, p. 127.
70. John J. Culley, "The Santa Fe Internment Camp and the Justice Program for Enemy Aliens," in Roger Daniels, Sandra C. Taylor, and Harry H. L. Kitano, eds., *Japanese Americans: From Relocation to Redress*. Seattle: University of Washington Press, 1986, p. 62.

Chapter 4: Creating Communities

71. Quoted in Smith, *Democracy on Trial*, p. 196.
72. Modell, *The Kikuchi Diary*, p. 135.
73. Uchida, *Desert Exile*, p. 89.

74. Modell, *The Kikuchi Diary*, p. 134.
75. Quoted in Tateishi, *And Justice for All*, p. 121.
76. Quoted in James, *Exile Within*, p. 61.
77. Quoted in Smith, *Democracy on Trial*, p. 202.
78. Uchida, *Desert Exile*, p. 97.
79. Uchida, *Desert Exile*, p. 85.
80. Weglyn, *Years of Infamy*, p. 105.
81. Modell, *The Kikuchi Diary*, pp. 124–25.
82. Quoted in Smith, *Democracy on Trial*, p. 258.
83. Modell, *The Kikuchi Diary*, p. 55.
84. Quoted in Tateishi, *And Justice for All*, p. 211.
85. Quoted in Tateishi, *And Justice for All*, p. 150.
86. Quoted in Smith, *Democracy on Trial*, p. 352.
87. Modell, *The Kikuchi Diary*, p. 230.
88. Quoted in Smith, *Democracy on Trial*, p. 354.
89. Weglyn, *Years of Infamy*, p. 98.

Chapter 5: Outside the Wire

90. Thomas Takeuchi, ed., *The Minidoka Interlude*. Hunt, ID: Published by the Residents of Minidoka Relocation Center, 1942–1943, p. 4.
91. Uchida, *Desert Exile*, p. 132.
92. Quoted in Smith, *Democracy on Trial*, p. 233.
93. Quoted in Daniels, *Prisoners Without Trial*, p. 79.
94. Uchida, *Desert Exile*, p. 115.
95. Quoted in Commission on Wartime Relocation, *Personal Justice Denied*, p. 182.
96. Quoted in Smith, *Democracy on Trial*, pp. 284–85.
97. Quoted in Tateishi, *And Justice for All*, p. 184.
98. Quoted in Daniel S. Davis, *Behind Barbed Wire*. New York: E. P. Dutton, 1982, pp. 103–104.
99. Quoted in Smith, *Democracy on Trial*, p. 392.
100. Quoted in Smith, *Democracy on Trial*, p. 275.

Chapter 6: Reaction to Betrayal

101. Quoted in Tateishi, *And Justice for All*, p. 106.
102. Quoted in Tateishi, *And Justice for All*, p. 70.
103. Quoted in Daniels, *Prisoners Without Trial*, p. 59.
104. Quoted in Daniels, *Concentration Camps U.S.A.*, p. 140.
105. Quoted in Daniels, *Prisoners Without Trial*, p. 63.
106. Uchida, *Desert Exile*, p. 132.
107. Modell, *The Kikuchi Diary*, p. 140.
108. Houston, *Farewell to Manzanar*, pp. 31–32.
109. Modell, *The Kikuchi Diary*, p. 82.
110. Modell, *The Kikuchi Diary*, p. 58.
111. Uchida, *Desert Exile*, p. 141.
112. Quoted in Commission on Wartime Relocation, *Personal Justice Denied*, p. 179.
113. Smith, *Democracy on Trial*, p. 292.
114. Quoted in Smith, *Democracy on Trial*, p. 339.
115. Quoted in Commission on Wartime Relocation, *Personal Justice Denied*, p. 197.
116. Quoted in Commission on Wartime Relocation, *Personal Justice Denied*, p. 196.
117. Quoted in Weglyn, *Years of Infamy*, p. 156.
118. Quoted in Smith, *Democracy on Trial*, p. 324.

119. Quoted in Commission on Wartime Relocation, *Personal Justice Denied*, p. 247.
120. Quoted in Weglyn, *Years of Infamy*, p. 216.
121. Weglyn, *Years of Infamy*, p. 233.
122. Quoted in Weglyn, *Years of Infamy*, p. 241.
123. Quoted in Weglyn, *Years of Infamy*, p. 240.
124. Quoted in Weglyn, *Years of Infamy*, p. 239.
125. Quoted in Weglyn, *Years of Infamy*, p. 247.

Chapter 7: Freedom!

126. Quoted in Armor and Wright, *Manzanar*, p. 60.
127. Quoted in Smith, *Democracy on Trial*, p. 369.
128. Quoted in Smith, *Democracy on Trial*, p. 371.
129. Quoted in Smith, *Democracy on Trial*, p. 373.
130. Quoted in Davis, *Behind Barbed Wire*, p. 128.
131. Quoted in Smith, *Democracy on Trial*, pp. 383–84.
132. Quoted in Tateishi, *And Justice for All*, p. 55.
133. Quoted in Smith, *Democracy on Trial*, p. 385.
134. Houston, *Farewell to Manzanar*, pp. 129–30.
135. Quoted in Smith, *Democracy on Trial*, p. 386.
136. Quoted in Weglyn, *Years of Infamy*, p. 265.
137. Quoted in Tateishi, *And Justice for All*, p. 145.
138. Quoted in Smith, *Democracy on Trial*, p. 401.
139. Testimony of Ayako Uyeda, taken from the *Hearing of U.S. Commission on Wartime Relocation and Internment of Civilians*, Seattle, WA, September 10, 1981, p. 34.
140. Tateishi, *And Justice for All*, p. vii.

Epilogue: Liberty and Justice for All

141. Commission on Wartime Relocation, *Personal Justice Denied*, p. 18.
142. Quoted in Daniels, *Prisoners Without Trial*, p. 102.
143. Weglyn, *Years of Infamy*, p. 267.
144. Tateishi, *And Justice for All*, p. xxvi.
145. Quoted in Tateishi, *And Justice for All*, p. 93.

For Further Reading

Daniel S. Davis, *Behind Barbed Wire*. New York: E. P. Dutton, 1982. Well-written account of Japanese American internment.

Jeanne Wakatsuki Houston and James D. Houston, *Farewell to Manzanar*. Boston: Houghton Mifflin, 1973. A first-person account of one Japanese American family interned at Manzanar.

Jerry Stanley, *I Am an American*. New York: Crown, 1994. Middle grade level. The story of the internment with many moving black-and-white photos.

Yoshiko Uchida, *Desert Exile*. Seattle: University of Washington Press, 1982. First-person account of a Japanese American family as told by the younger daughter. Easy to read, hard to put down.

Works Consulted

John Armor and Peter Wright, *Manzanar.* New York: Times Books, 1988. An account of life in Manzanar Relocation Center, with photos by photojournalist Ansel Adams and a commentary by renowned author John Hersey.

Commission on Wartime Relocation and Internment of Civilians, *Personal Justice Denied.* Washington: GPO, 1982. The definitive government report on internment, compiled almost forty years after the fact.

Roger Daniels, *Concentration Camps U.S.A.* New York: Holt, Rinehart & Winston, 1972. Focuses on the political aspects of internment from Pearl Harbor to resettlement.

————, *Prisoners Without Trial.* New York: Hill & Wang, 1993. A brief but excellent account of the Japanese American experience by an expert on the history of Asian immigration.

Roger Daniels, Sandra C. Taylor, and Harry H. L. Kitano, eds., *Japanese Americans: From Relocation to Redress.* Seattle: University of Washington Press, 1986. A selection of articles that range from discussion of the evacuation order to debate over redress and reparations after internment.

Anne Reeploeg Fisher, *Exile of A Race.* Seattle: F. & T. Publishers, 1965. History of Japanese American internment, including excerpts from newspapers, magazines, and congressional hearings.

Hearing of U.S. Commission on Wartime Relocation and Internment of Civilians, Seattle, WA, September 10, 1981. Records of testimony heard by a postwar federal commission during its investigation of internment.

Thomas James, *Exile Within.* Cambridge, MA: Harvard University Press, 1987. Complete account of government and internee efforts to educate children in the camps.

Eric D. Johnson, "'Quiet Americans' Remember Pain," *Pierce County Herald,* October 1, 1985. Former internees living in Washington State remember the trauma of internment and their experiences after the war.

Daisuke Kitagawa, *Issei and Nisei: The Internment Years.* New York: Seabury Press, 1967. First-person account of life in Tule Lake Relocation Center including the author's experiences reentering mainstream society in the East.

John Modell, ed., *The Kikuchi Diary.* Urbana: University of Illinois Press, 1973. Excerpts from the journal of college student Charles Kikuchi, beginning with Pearl Harbor and continuing through his months of internment at the Tanforan Assembly Center in California.

Page Smith, *Democracy on Trial.* New York: Simon & Schuster, 1995. A detailed and well-written account of internment, sprinkled with quotes from the internees themselves.

Thomas Takeuchi, ed., *The Minidoka Interlude*. Hunt, ID: Published by the Residents of Minidoka Relocation Center, 1942–1943. A photo-essay of life in the Idaho center, complete with group photos of residents, candid snapshots of camp activities, and upbeat comments on camp life, edited by one of its internees.

John Tateishi, *And Justice for All*. New York: Random House, 1984. Short, moving narratives written by former internees.

Michi Weglyn, *Years of Infamy*. New York: William Morrow, Quill Paperbacks, 1976. The story of Japanese American internment camps written by a former internee. Includes disturbing information on conditions at Tule Lake Segregation Center for "disloyal" internees.

Index

Picture Credits

Cover photo: FPG International
AP/Wide World Photos, 24, 25, 27, 31, 32, 34, 87, 94
Archive Photos, 14
California State Library, 13
Corbis-Bettmann, 55
Library of Congress, 8, 29, 65

National Archives, 10, 21, 26, 41
National Japanese American Historical Society, 16, 18, 37, 38, 39, 40, 42, 43, 45, 48 (both), 49, 51, 54, 60, 61, 62, 63, 68, 70, 71, 83, 89, 90, 91
UPI/Corbis-Bettmann, 9, 15, 17, 35, 36, 56, 58, 67, 72, 75, 76, 82, 97

About the Author

Diane Yancey began writing for her own entertainment when she was thirteen, living in Grass Valley, California. Later she graduated from Augustana College in Illinois. She now pursues a writing career in the Pacific Northwest, where she lives with her husband, two daughters, and two cats. Her interests include collecting old books, building miniature houses, and traveling.

Ms. Yancey's books include *Desperadoes and Dynamite*, *The Reunification of Germany*, *The Hunt for Hidden Killers*, *Life in War-Torn Bosnia*, *Camels for Uncle Sam*, and *Life in the Elizabethan Theater*.